The History of Miss Melmoth. In two Volumes. By the Author of The Fine Lady. ... of 2

THE

HISTORY

OF

MISS MELMOTH.

IN TWO VOLUMES

By the AUTHOR of the FINE LADY.

VOL. I.

"Let Emma's hapless case be falsely told,
"By the rash young, or the ill-natur'd old,
"Let every tongue its various censures chuse,
"Acquit with coldness, or with spite accuse
"Fair Truth at last her radiant head shall raise,
"And malice vanquish'd heighten Virtue's praise
     PRIOR's Henry and Emma

DUBLIN

PRINTED FOR JAMES WILLIAMS, AT No 5,
SKINNER-ROW MDCCLXXII

THE
HISTORY
OF
MISS MELMOTH.

LETTER I.

To EDWARD GRENVILLE, Efq,

Bruton-Street, May 25.

MY vifits, fince I have been in town, have been chiefly confined to Mrs Grafton's Houfe. My intimacy with her late nephew, has made me almoſt part of the family. Tho' to own the truth fairly and honeſtly, I went thither frequently in the hope of feeing Miſs Melmoth, who has been long expected from Vere-Park.

Miſs Grafton feems to honour me with fome particular marks of efteem, which have however made no impreſſion on the heart of your friend. one prefervative may be, the little affection fhe was known to have for our worthy Grafton, who certainly merited all the love in the power of a fifter to beſtow. He indeed never much talked on the fubject, but from hints, I gathered enough to learn fhe did not behave as he wifhed—or deferved.

This afternoon being Mrs Grafton's Rout, I dreſt myſelf to attend the card-table ſummons. When I entered the drawing-room, my eyes were inſtantly attracted by the moſt lovely figure I ever beheld. As moſt of the company were engaged in parties, I had time to contemplate this charming creature, who was ſtanding behind Lady Darnly's Chair. Her dreſs was a white ſpotted luſtring negligée. Her lovely auburn hair without powder, gloſſy as ſatin. A face inclined to the oval, perfectly fair, made the moſt pleaſing contraſt to her charming, dark hazle eyes, and long laſhes. Her eye-brows beautifully arched. And when ſhe ſpoke, or ſmiled, the ſweeteſt dimples play'd in her cheeks and mouth. In ſhort, it was impoſſible to behold an object ſo engaging, without being ſenſibly ſtruck with her charms, which, however, ſhe ſeemed not at all to be conſcious of herſelf. So far from taking viſible pleaſure in the ſoft ſpeeches I obſerved the Beaux pour in her ear, as moſt of the young giddy flirts do, ſhe paid only a barely civil attention to them. I ſhould be an age in enumerating the beauties of this lovely girl. One thing however I muſt obſerve, ſhe had that delicate ſoft languor in her eyes, which men in general, and you and I in particular admire.

> Her beauteous cheeks the bluſh of Venus wear,
> Chaſten'd by coy Diana's penſive air.

Among the number of belles preſent, it was impoſſible, tho' I had heard Miſs Melmoth was expected, to be certain which was that young lady.—While my eyes feaſted themſelves, I could not but breathe a wiſh, this might be the fair one I was longing to ſee. But whether ſhe proved

proved fo or not, I found would make little difference.

As foon as an opportunity prefented itfelf to fpeak to Mifs Grafton, which was as foon as fhe could difengage herfelf from a party, to come to me, I queftioned her of the lovely ftranger. Not that I gave her that epithet, no, no, Ned, I do know better than that too. I afked in a carelefs degagée manner, who that lady, fituated as before defcribed, was. O how my heart bounded when fhe anfwered "Mifs Melmoth." I am willing to attribute my emotions at the time, to the partiality my friend Grafton had for this amiable girl, but it is certain I never felt fuch emotion before, at the fight of any woman. If it is the beginning of love, I profefs. But love at firft fight too. I am not fingular however.

I cannot figure to myfelf a more exquifite happinefs than the poffeffion of fuch a lovely woman's heart. What permanent felicity would accrue to me, could I flatter myfelf I may hereafter touch her's! It fhall from this moment be my ftudy to deferve her.

Tho' Mrs Grafton is the beft of women, yet a ftate of dependence, which is this divine creature's fituation, cannot be pleafing. The mind muft endure fome difagreeable fenfations. Perhaps the air of langour I remarked, may be owing to this, and Mifs Grafton may not act with the fame obliging tendernefs as her aunt. O what tranfporting joy, to difpel every cloud of uneafinefs from her lovely brow, and place love, and lafting happinefs there!

My dear Grenville, you will think me far gone indeed, to be fo taken by the heart through the eyes, but you are miftaken. I converfed with her upon various topics. All which fhe difcuffed with such perspicuity and modest judgment, as truly charmed me.

If her mother was half as amiable, Melmoth was a villain not to marry her; for Miss Grafton assured me last night, she was natural daughter to her uncle. That intelligence is however different from Harry Grafton's, who told me she was an orphan left in distress tho', upon reflection, Mr Melmoth might raise such a report in order to throw a veil over his guilt. He left her intirely dependent on his sister Mrs Grafton, an unfatherly part; for is she not as much his child, as if the priest had joined his hand to her mother's? and in equity ought to have shared his fortunes.

I find I shall not be able to avoid paying a visit or two at Mrs. Grafton's. Perhaps prudence will suggest, I ought not to go thither; but something stronger than prudence impels me.

Saturday I propose setting out for Evelin-Abbey. Her ladyship presses my return. She fondly tells me my presence constitutes her happiness. I will chearfully obey her summons; when did I with regret? I have more obligations to Lady Evelin than it is in the power of man to repay. With what unremitting tenderness did she watch over my earliest years! too soon deprived of a beloved husband, she devoted all her widowed state to the education of her only child. Amiable, beloved parent! shall I deprive thee of the only blessing thou sayst thou canst now enjoy? Forbid it gratitude!

My dearest Grenville, when you can leave your uncle, I expect to see you at the Abbey: my mother too expects you. In her last letter she says, she would not so strenuously intreat (she never commands) me to come to her, only that I
shall

shall sooner enjoy the company of my Grenville
I hope your uncle's gout will leave you and him
at liberty—He to follow his hounds and you, the
impulses of your affection, which I doubt not will
lead you to the Abbey, and
Your faithful
JOHN EVELIN

LETTER II

To Miss SIDNEY VERE

Grosvenor-Square, May 25

THE Fates are determined to make you a false prophetess, Sidney. Where are the beaux by dozens, which you pretended to see by inspiration falling at my feet; and rattling their chains in rustic harmony? Nothing of all this I assure you has happened: with grief I tell you, I fear never will; for I have not had the supreme delight yet of striking one swain dead by a frown, or raising him to life again by a smile. Hard fate this! is it not? But here is a fresh importation of beaux I can tell you—Among the rest, Lord L———. O Sidney! I remember the time when I thought it impossible to hear that name mentioned without emotion. Ah, with what fervency I loved the charming youth! Ha! ha! ha! Do you not recollect, what tender glances used to fly from one to t'other? I hope he has quite forgot our childish attachment; tho' I then thought myself woman enough to inspire the most ardent passion in the breast of my Oroondates. I, in my thirteenth year, he almost sixteen. What a pair of soft, sighing, weeping Lovers we were! I really think, I never experienced so much felicity in

any moment of my life, and I am sure, never half
the triumph, as when we were invited to old
Lord M——'s, on his nephew's birth-day.—Upon my word, he was a beautiful youth. How
elegantly he looked in his silver cloaths! I no less
so, as he told me, in my silver-tissue robe with
pink flowers. But when I was chosen queen of
the feast, and opened the ball with my lover, a
term you may remember I was particularly fond
of, O how I was envied by all the little Misses
of my own age! Mercy on me! how have I run
on about my first love! But I have proved incon-
stant, and he has had a thousand since; indeed I
have heard, he lived a very gay life abroad.

Your request, my Sidney, I think was, that I
should give you an account of the people I see,
the diversions I am present at, and in short, every
thing that happens to fall in my way. You have
not before you a very fine prospect in my correspondence; but I judge of you according to my
own feelings; every trifle from my Sidney is pleasing to me; your partiality for your Caroline will
render her letters so to you. My first contained
only thanks to your dear mama, for her kindness
to her Sidney's friend, and the tender reception I
received from my more than parent. This has not
much to boast of, as I have not yet seen any body,
—the Darnly family excepted. Lady Darnly has
taken very polite notice of me. The young ladies
renewed friendship with me, and laid claim to
more. I believe I shall not be able, or willing to
refuse it to them. We dined with them yesterday.
They were alone. Sir George broke thro' an appointment that he might have the pleasure of seeing
your Caroline. He made me many compliments,
undeserved, I fear; yet not frothy, as the men too
frequently are——Company is expected this afternoon,

ternoon, an assembly my benefactress gives into every fashionable amusement. I must leave off to dress for the occasion, and am,

with great sincerity,
my beloved Sidney's faithful
CAROLINE MELMOTH.

LETTER III.

To Miss VERE.

Grosvenor-Square, May 30.

MANY thanks to my dear Sidney, for her sweet letter *. You have given me a subject. You was too young when you saw Sir George Dainly, to remember his person now. And you request a description of him from me, for two reasons: first, because you have heard he is very handsome, and secondly, because you love my descriptive talent. I fear, my dear, I shall neither do justice to his merit or your opinion. Words do not at any time, I think, convey an adequate idea of a handsome person, for tho' you can tell the colour of the complexion and eyes, yet it is impossible to paint the bloom of one, or the brilliancy of the other. However, it will be more polite in me to execute your commission by halves, than not at all; therefore I will begin.

Sir George Dainly is above the middle size, not too tall, tho' you know I do not like your violent tall men. I cannot tell you how many feet he measures, but, I should suppose, about five feet, eight or nine. They lay the standard height of a man is six feet; but tho' Sir George reaches not so high, I believe no one will dispute his being the most graceful figure that can be seen. I
looked

* Miss Vere's letter is omitted.

looked at him as attentively as I durst, in order to satisfy your curiosity as much as possible, and tho' I beheld him with the most scrutinizing eye, I could not discover one feature which was not perfect. His hair is chesnut colour. His eyebrows and lashes, both the finest I ever saw, black. But his eyes—There is no doing justice to his eyes. I never beheld such lustre in any one's, man or woman. His forehead is as fine as you can imagine, and contrasted with his eye-brows make the upper part of his face truly pleasing.

He generally wears his hair dress'd in the present mode, but not rais'd high at top. His nose is a little aquiline, finely turned! His mouth, in my eyes, is rendered charming, from a projection of his under-lip, yet not to give the appearance of what is called, being under-hung; but it looks, as Suckling says, as if "some bee had stung it newly." Teeth perfectly even, and white as snow. You, Sidney, would be in love with him had he no other charm than the sweetest dimple, when he smiles, in his left cheek. The men agree in his being exactly proportioned. This is a pretty accurate description. I hope you are satisfied: and yet, I do not think you can put all these features and limbs together, so as to produce that harmony—apropos! of harmony, his voice in common speaking is sweetly melodious.

He has a manner of looking sometimes as would make a stranger think him very proud, [by the bye, there is a great deal of the *hauteur* in the family] but yet I wish you could see the very look I have described, it is to me, infinitely graceful.

After this, I shall not draw any one's picture; as it would only be looking at a common dauber's painting, after you had contemplated a Guido. Now,

Now, will you not think I have given my heart to this Adonis? no, my dear, it is very safe, and I hope will long continue so. Friendship is enough for me. Bleſt with my Sidney, life is a treaſure, and I have no room for love. I may cultivate a friendſhip tho', with this man, beloved as I am by his neareſt relations. It would gratify one's vanity much, to be eſteemed by a man ſo univerſally admired as Sir George is, by all who know him. His ſiſters want him to marry. Louiſa thinks there is ſome lady abroad he likes, ſhe hinted as if Lord Wilton ſaid ſo. I wonder who ſhe is. How happy muſt ſhe be, my dear Sidney, whoever ſhe be, to inſpire ſuch a man with love, to change that air of haughtineſs to gentle languor and tender ſoftneſs!

I have not ſaid a word of the intellectual man, nor would there be any neceſſity were you to ſee him; but as you have not had that happineſs, I will only tell you, he has improved the fineſt natural genius in the world, by every acquirement which a large fortune and a thirſt of knowledge could procure.

I would make my letter longer, but I know not how to deſcend from my altitudes; therefore muſt drop on a ſudden. Adieu, my deareſt Sidney.

    Ever your's,
     CAROLINE MELMOTH.

I muſt add further, before my letter goes to the poſt, Lady Darnley has begged Mrs Grafton's permiſſion to take me into the country, in about a fortnight. Sir George is to be of the party. He is a great reader; how charmingly ſhall we paſs our hours!

LETTER IV.

To Miss MELMOTH.

Vere-Park, June 2.

GIVEN your heart! No it would be abfolutely ridiculous to fuppofe fuch a thing. Whence could fuch a fuggeſtion arife? Could you imagine I fhould ever fufpect it? Who would wifh to lofe their heart to fuch a man, when they may hope for his friendfhip and efteem, and befides, when there is a lady abroad, who muſt be the happieſt creature on *terra firma!* But how in the name of confiftency, can you judge the happinefs this fair lady will experience?—Ah Caroline! Caroline!—You hold your fan before your eyes, and I may not have a peep between the fticks. But I'll punifh you for your difingenuity. And as a proof of my intentions, and as an earneft, I will not write a word more of this *Rara Avis* yet upon fecond thoughts, which the wife fay are always beſt——I will too, as the topic is one fo totally indifferent to you, you know. Why yes, as you fay, a pretty fellow to read to one in a rainy morning, is very well, when they have fenfe to chufe a proper fubject fomething foft and tender, is it fo Caroline? And then if he enters into the fpirit of the piece, and fhould chance to fix his eyes on you—" eyes that beggar all defcription"——they may pofſibly melt into that foft languor you fo much wifh to fee. Ha! ha! ha! what pains have you taken to deceive yourfelf and me! Whether you have fucceeded in the firft, I know not, tho' I fhould, for your fenfibility-fake, rather hope the contrary but in the fecond part,

you

you were never more miſtaken in your life. Lord, my dear, I would aſk a child of three years old, who Caroline Melmoth loved, and if it did not point its finger to Sir George Darnley, I would whip the little brat ſoundly. Had you repeated, what you have written, in a wood, each bird on the ſpray would have told it was love that prompted your elaborate deſcription.

Your attempting to conceal your paſſion, is like holding a priſm before a candle; you obſtruct the immediate body of light, 'tis true, but it throws out a thouſand different rays, and the effulgence of its beams is the ſame.

Well, ſeriouſly tho', I think your ſecond Love, I cry your mercy, Friend, I mean, as far tranſcends your firſt, as the ſun does the moon. I have heard a ſtrange ſtory or two lately of his Lordſhip, and not more ſtrange than true, I believe. He is, I am told, a very ſpecious man, therefore, a dangerous one. I ought to ſay a great deal to guard you againſt his attacks, ſhould he be inclined to renew the childiſh play between you; for as your heart is ſo totally indifferent to every one, and perfectly diſengaged, there is ſome room for apprehenſions; but I will rely on your known prudence.—Heaven ſend, and preſerve, all happineſs to you! May the man be worthy of my beloved Caroline!

I ſuppoſe I ſhall not hear often from you, while at Darnley-Grove, as your time will be a good deal taken up. If you can beſtow a moment on me before you ſet out, you will eternally oblige

Your ever devoted

SIDNEY VERF

LETTER

LETTER V.

To Miss Vere.

Grosvenor Square, June 4.

AMONG the swains who visit here, is Sir John Evelin. A most amiable young man! Rich, handsome, wise, discreet, and a number of other requisites. He was an intimate friend of young Mr Grafton's, who used to speak highly of him, in his letters to his aunt. The first time I saw Sir John, was at a Rout here. He took an opportunity of chatting a good deal with me. I liked his conversation extremely. We talked on many subjects, and he seemed perfect master of all. You know, I chuse in general to be rather of the hearing, than speaking part, but he drew me in, to talk more, than perhaps I ought, it was owing, I believe, to his great modesty, which gave me courage.

Miss Grafton, from the frequent visits he paid here, before I came to town, has set him down for an admirer, but I own, I think his conduct contradicts her opinion. I wish he was; but am afraid she does not build upon very sure grounds.

But I forget, you rally me on my elaborate description of Sir George Darnley. I am in love! Ridiculous! No, no, Sidney, you were never more mistaken. How could such a surmise enter your imagination? I would give you the picture of Sir John Evelin, but you would infer from my praise, that I am in love with him too. Take care, Sidney, if ever I catch you, I will have no mercy. Remember my threat, and tremble at the

the consequences, preserve your heart free from love Be mine wholly; as I am, and ever will be, yours,——But, did I really paint the perfections of Sir George Darnley in such glowing colours? I know not if I did I wish you were to see him, then would you allow I had not done him justice

Lord L—— visits here frequently he seems prodigiously assiduous to Miss Grafton There is something in her very attractive The Men all seem to admire her You won't allow her to be handsome I think her infinitely so, and very agreeable If we differ in this point, I know no other in which we do I am most pleased with myself, when I think like you You cannot imagine, Sidney, how happy I am, that Lord L—— takes no notice of our childish folly He behaves with great politeness, but is in my mind amazingly altered He is, in short, a man I do not like

My benefactress has made Miss Grafton and myself a most elegant present of jewels which were to have been worn to-day, but the celebration of his Majesty's birth-day is put off, on account of the mourning

In themselves, you, who know me, will believe, the diamonds could give me no pleasure but the satisfaction I experience, in receiving the meerest trifle from my ever kind patroness, is inexpressible. Ought I to repine, my dearest Sidney, at my destiny; which has brought me to the knowledge of the most worthy of women, and the friendship of my beloved Miss Vere; the dearest, truest of friends? am I not a happy girl?

Lady Darnley proposes setting out for the Grove the beginning of the week I shall have some affairs to settle, as the time is shorter than was first talked of.

Will

Will not your mama, my love, spare you to come to me, when I return to Grosvenor-Square? Mrs Grafton joins with me to request that favour——Do tell me in your next, you will oblige

your faithful
CAROLINE MELMOTH.

LETTER VI.

To Miss VERE.

Darnley-Grove, June 20.

HOW charming is every scene here! It is the sweetest spot in the world. But, as the day proves a rainy one, I will not keep you out of doors, but introduce you into the garden parlour where you will find, engaged in pleasing and instructive conversation, Lady Darnley, her two daughters, Lord Wilton, Sir George, and your Caroline.

Lord Wilton is an amiable man, but Lord Wilton is not happy.——I have lately learned some particulars of his life, chiefly from his own lips.

At the age of twenty, a tyrannical father left him the cruel alternative, of marrying a woman he hated, or being disinherited. All the tears and prayers of an only child made no impression on the obdurate heart of an inexorable parent. As his last subterfuge, Lord Wilton formed the resolution to address the lady. He acquainted her with his invincible compunction to an union, where there was so little prospect of happiness, and in the most urgent manner represented the misery of being for

life

life united to a woman he could not love, and the inexpreſſible anguiſh ſhe muſt endure, in giving her heart and hand to a man, who was incapable of repaying her tenderneſs. Would ſhe but, in pity to him and herſelf, relinquiſh her former views, ſhe would lay claim to his utmoſt gratitude. She heard him—'tis true; but inſtead of availing herſelf of the information he gave her, to leave perſecuting an unhappy youth, and in the end making herſelf miſerable, ſhe immediately went to his father, and acquainted him with the ſentiments of his ſon. The conſequences were, his obliging his unhappy ſon, directly to receive the hand of this baſe woman, or quit the houſe, deprived of all future hope of ſubſiſtence, and labouring under a heavy anathema from his enraged father. The unfortunate Lord Wilton was thus made a victim to the licentious paſſion of a vile woman; for could her attachment merit a better title? certainly not.

Lord Wilton's former diſlike encreaſed to the moſt inſurmountable averſion; which the conduct of his wife augmented every day. She found herſelf diſappointed, in the hope he would, (when their marriage was over, and an impoſſibility of again being free) remit the coldneſs, with which he treated her——He ſpent whole days in hunting and ſhooting, to avoid the company of Lady Wilton. His only conſolation was, his not preferring any other woman, though he could not avoid thinking every woman he converſed with would have made him happier, than her who had fallen to his lot.

How inexpreſſibly miſerable muſt be the ſituation of Lord Wilton! With a heart formed with the utmoſt ſenſibility, tenderly ſuſceptible of
the

the woes of others, how must he feel! how lament his own!

Lady Wilton wanted delicacy, sense, and many other requisites. Her sentiments diametrically opposite to her husband's. Her ideas were unrefined. She entertained a number of servile flatterers, who grossly indulged her vanity, and felt-adulation. No wonder Wilton-Grange so seldom saw its master. After few years unremitting torment, the death of his father left Lord Wilton more at liberty. As soon as he could settle his affairs, he left the place which had too long been the scene of his misery.

In London a life of dissipation first presented itself to Lord Wilton's view; but to a man of his sentiments, such a life could not be long pleasing. He easily got into action to families of his own rank. Persons of his figure and address are seldom rejected. Had he been a man of *gallantry*, in the present acceptation of the word, he might have boasted with Cæsar, that he " came, saw, and " overcame." But Lord Wilton is a man of honor.

His acquaintance with Sir George Darnley, at Oxford, rendered an introduction to the family very practicable. Every body knew Lord Wilton was unhappily married, and that he lived in a state of separation from his wife, yet no father, no husband, were uneasy, when he was engaged in conversation with a daughter or wife.

His person is noble, tall, manly, tender, graceful. His hair, a fine light brown, fair complexion, and blue eyes. His address perfectly amiable, and a heart filled with the most noble sentiments of honor.

Lord Wilton has now resided in town about two years. he often talked of going to Italy, but is constrained, I fear, by a fatal attachment (which augments his misery) to stay.

Deserving as he is, I see him unhappy—ah! must he not still remain so? He walks with us, reads to us, and is quite our companion, Sir George is so likewise. After breakfast we assemble—when too hot to walk—in the most delightful summer retreat you can form an idea of. It is a room open to the garden (from whence it takes the appellation of the garden-parlour) by folding-doors, and large windows; on a terrace at a little distance are trees planted, which shade it from the sun, and the spaces between are filled with orange, lemon, and myrtle-trees, all in bloom. There we females take our different work, the two gentlemen fix upon a book they think most proper to convey instruction, at the same time it amuses. They read by turns, and we each give our separate sentiments on the subject. Many improving observations may be gathered from both the gentlemen. I said, *we* give our sentiments, for they oblige me sometimes to give my opinion, which I never do unasked, but I think it would be a ridiculous affectation of diffidence, were I to refuse when called upon. Sir George most kindly sets me right, if he thinks I have got beyond my depth in any point, but manages it so, that I have the praise of every one for my discernment, at the same time all the merit is his; my thoughts coincide with his, but I have not his manner of expressing myself.

But this is a digression from what I was before relating.

Lord Wilton for some days has appeared melancholy; he sighs when the conversation takes a general turn, he will, when addressed, seem wholly lost; and unacquainted with the subject.

It

It is impossible to know Lord Wilton, without feeling a compassion for him. You know I am of a serious turn; he will very often, therefore, when we are walking, single me out, and enter upon some grave conversation. He always leaves me melancholy. I am certain he loves. Ah, how dreadful that passion! how destructive to the peace of human minds! how seldom does it conduce to our happiness!

I will not, my dearest Sidney, finish my letter now, as I may have something more to tell you by-and-b

June 22.

Bless me! my dear, Lord Wilton has just now, in a whisper, begged I will favour him with a few moments conversation in the grove. He has something of the utmost consequence to reveal to me—what can it be? I am terrified to death!—good God! should he have conceived a passion for me—I am sure he is under the influence of a passion—what shall I do?—How unhappy has his mysterious behaviour made me!—How I long, yet dread, to give him the requested meeting. For the world's wealth, I would not be the object of Lord Wilton's love; for with all his accomplishments, were he a free man, he would, he could be nothing to me. I think I behold all men with equal indifference—But the time draws near. I must quit my pen, and prepare to meet him.

Eight o'Clock.

Lord Wilton was punctual. "He thanked me "for my condescension, in complying with his "request; which" he said, "he should have "made before, but from the dread of giving me "pain." This was an interesting beginning——

He

He gave a melancholy recital of his situation. " the unhappiness of which" he said " was much " augmented, from his being too sensible of the " merit of one of the most amiable of women "— As this is the phrase of the men, I trembled left he meant me---I was silent---he continued and eased my fears, by confessing " he had long beheld " Miss Darnley with admiration but since his " more intimate knowledge of her worth, he " found his flame too great to be concealed, un- " less he fled from the danger He knew not " how to act,—begged I would advise him. He " would not form a wish, that Louisa might be " acquainted with his unhappy passion, and yet, " should she give her hand to another, he should " be the most miserable of men "——I never saw a man so distressed Good God! how was grief painted on his countenance! I knew not what to advise him To have given him hope, would have been very imprudent, where there is so little foundation for any. I strove, by every argument, to enable him to support his evil destiny, he owned the justice of them, " and sincerely thanked me " for my goodness, in endeavouring to comfort " him but he could not support the idea of any " one's possessing Miss Darnley "

I told him, " I believed hitherto, Louisa had no " partiality for any man that she very highly es- " teemed his lordship, and that whenever I found " a lover of Miss Darnley's very importunate, I " would, in as delicate a manner as possible, ac- " quaint her, she had for the sincerest admirer " one of the most worthy of men " and concluded with " wishing him all happiness." adding " he " might depend on my best services Heaven only " knew how I pitied him " Lord Wilton kissed
my

my hand with rapture "Beft of women!" faid
he, "if you pity, I muft be happy! Heaven re-
"ward you for your goodnefs to me!"

He begged I would fpeak favorably of him, as
opportunity fhould ferve "it might be the means
"of ftrengthening the efteem Mifs Darnley in-
"dulged for him Yet," added he, "ought I to
"wifh that charming creature fhould feel too
"great an efteem for me? I know not what I
"ought to do I am wretched myfelf, but can
"not, dare not, involve the woman I love more
"than life, in my diftrefs." Do you not revere
Lord Wilton, my Sidney? what an amiable, yet
unhappy man he is!

He fays, "he fhall be troublefome to me, he
"fears, as he now takes all opportunities of be-
"ing at my fide Since he has opened his heart
"to me, he is much eafier yet fays he ought not
"to difturb my repofe, by his intrufive melan-
"choly" I re-affured him, "how fenfibly I
"felt for him that my heart bled for his dif-
"treffes" He takes pleafure now in talking of
his paffion but is that the way to cure it? It
would be cruel to undeceive him, by recommend-
ing abfence ——Poor Lord Wilton! how dreadful
is this fame paffion of love! O, may my acquaintance with it be only from the experience of others!

Lord Wilton and Sir George hunt fometimes,
and we lofe them for the whole day We pafs our
time, I know not how, rather infipidly, when they
are abfent we feem to have loft fomething which
our utmoft endeavours cannot procure

June 24

My good Mrs Grafton has not yet fent me a
fummons I fhould be ungrateful to my friends
here, were I to fay I wifh to be in town,
and

and to Mrs. Grafton, if I did not obey her firſt ſummons chearfully.

June 25.

Lord Wilton talks of leaving us very ſoon. He tells me, "he muſt fly." He dares not truſt himſelf longer "in the preſence of the amiable object of his love." His paſſion is all purity. What has not his father to anſwer for! A man, ſo calculated for a domeſtic and ſocial life! All his fair proſpects blaſted! Formed to make happy a woman of Miſs Darnley's taſte. Their ſentiments naturally coincide upon every occaſion. How bleſt they might have been! And what a dreadful reverſe preſents itſelf! For I firmly believe, Louiſa but too ſenſibly does juſtice to Lord Wilton's merit.

His abſence is now talked of in the family. Sir George intends to accompany his friend to Dover. We ſhall therefore loſe him for near, if not altogether a week. I fancy we ſhall not paſs our time very agreeably in that ſpace.

Never mother and ſiſters loved a ſon or brother, more than Lady Darnly, and her daughters, do Sir George. or with more reaſon, I would ſay, were you not too ready to draw inferences, which have no foundation but in your inventive brain.

I ſhall write no more 'till our Beaux are departed. This letter is journalwiſe as I have not had time to write much together. Adieu, my deareſt Sidney, believe me

Ever your's,

CAROLINE MELMOTH.

LETTER VII

To Miss VERE.

Darnley-Grove, June 29

THE day is arrived on which Lord Wilton is to take leave. He last night gave me a letter, wherein he reiterates all he had before urged a thousand times, and begs the continuation of the friendship I now profess for him. Poor Lord Wilton! what anguish must he endure! Louisa too is much to be pitied. How happy would she have been, had she known him free, had it fallen to her lot to have captivated such a man!

Many people censure Lord Wilton, for not keeping up appearances with his wife to the world. But do not those censures evince the propensity the world has to encourage hypocrisy? Lord Wilton acted with honour and sincerity, when he declared to Miss Savage he never could love her. His conduct has ever been uniform, and consistent [in my humble opinion] with the sentiments of a man of true honour. I can never believe that oath, which we are constrained to take, is binding; it cannot be—

Cut off in my reasonings by the breakfast bell. It will be a melancholy meeting, so soon to part. Adieu, my Sidney, 'till the separation is over.

Twelve o'Clock.

They are gone, my Sidney. Ah, how affectingly aweful is the parting with those we esteem. Lord Wilton addressed us severally, in a most pathetic manner. He intreated to have a place in my memory, and added some things, intelligible

ble only to ourselves. He spoke least to Louisa; but looked in one glance, a thousand tender soft adieus. After saluting us, he hurried away, to conceal emotions, too visible in his expressive countenance. Sir George followed his example. I am almost ashamed, Sidney, to tell you the perturbation I experienced when he took his leave. Perhaps it was owing to my spirits being lowered by the solemnity of our parting with Lord Wilton, or, to my never having received a salute from him before, or to the ardor of it, for he did not touch my cheek as is usual, but actually pressed my lips. I felt my color come and go. I trembled—looked like a fool, I am sure, and involuntarily dropped a courtesy, as if to thank him for all favors. —But this is not the only circumstance that alarms me. Surely, surely, your predictions are not true. I think, Sidney, you were never in love, was you? You say you never loved Archer. Mordaunt you could not love.———I must reflect a little.

Two o'Clock.

I comforted myself, or rather flattered myself, my uneasiness was owing wholly to the departure of Lord Wilton, and my participation of his distress; but I feel a kind of consciousness when I attempt to name Sir George. You will miss my brother, said Harriot, just now, in your fishing parties. Why did I blush? Why endeavour to conceal my blushing confusion? I unknowingly strayed into the walk most frequented by Sir George, seated myself in the chair in which he had been placed. Nay, I once caught myself entering the garden parlour, and sighed, because it wanted its chief ornament. My feet insensibly led me into the picture-gallery. my eyes immediately adhered to his portrait, and unbidden tears wandered

wandered down my cheeks. Ay, Sidney! I can no longer hide it from myself: he is too, too amiable, and your friend is undone. it must be so.—Why did Mrs Grafton permit me to pay a visit to Darnley-Grove?—Ah, how calculated for my undoing! To spend whole days in his society —Continually to behold his graceful person,— to listen to his harmonious voice,—to—But do not laugh at me, my Sidney; it is not surely so unnatural! Every thing in this bewitching place conspired to the conquest of my poor inexperienced heart. Softened by the repetition of Lord Wilton's distress, I fancied I sighed for him. But, ah! I then admitted for an inmate, a passion perhaps destructive to my future peace.

Miss Darnley is very melancholy: she each moment laments the absence of her brother, while I repeat how much we miss Lord Wilton.

June 30, Nine o'Clock in the Evening.

Have a little mercy on me, my dear Sidney, as I so freely lay my heart, with all its follies, before you. May I not claim some little merit for my explicitness, in shewing you the most retired sentiments of my bosom, as soon as I became acquainted with them myself? For 'till this absence, I knew not, that the inexpressible pleasure, I felt in beholding Sir George, had any other source than friendship for the family authorised.—Alas! I never reflected, that friendship with the other sex is closely allied to love.

The evil I prayed against, is now befallen me. Help me, assist me, my most valued friend, either to extricate myself from the evil, or to support me under it.

I have made a thousand resolutions and attempts, since I discovered the state of my heart, to eradicate this tenderness from it. nay, I once fancied

I had

I had gained a complete victory, and put all my sensibility to flight. Ah! how weak the victory! In the midst of my boasted triumph, a line of a song, I had heard Sir George sing, obtruded itself to my recollection, and sighing, I repeated "Ah! " why should love, with tyrant sway, oppress " each youthful heart!" A tear of sympathy bore testimony to the succeeding lines.

I love! my Sidney, I know I feel I do in its full force. But with what hope!—I believe indeed, he has an esteem for me, perhaps a partiality; but I am not vain enough to suppose he is in love with me.

Notwithstanding the little probability, [possibility, I might have said] of my ever reaping the least emolument from my passion, I fear I must now term it so, yet I feel—I experience a kind of satisfaction, to which I was a stranger before.

There is, some-how, a sort of vacuity in our hearts, which friendship alone cannot fill. Even my firm attachment to you prevented not a void in my bosom. Love was certainly given us to constitute our greatest felicity.

I tacitly congratulate myself, on my being so sensible of Sir George Darnley's abundant merit. But these you will call mere trifling evasions, of what I cannot justify. You perhaps will say I am mad, to indulge a partiality for a man, between whom, and myself, the disparity is so obvious——Ah, spare me, my Sidney! Do not place my situation in too humiliating a light. I am but too sensible of my inferiority.

Were the advantages on my side, I would with joy convince the world, I beheld and revered such merit as must be conspicuous to every one (tho' so few will allow it is due reward.) With what rapture, were I an empress, would I raise him to share my empire, as he already does my heart!

I repeat to myself every speech which I can recollect, that seems to have any tenderness in it, as they fell from the lips of the most lovely of men, each look, each action too. Then with a transport, which fills my soul, and lifts me above the world, I silently dwell upon these recollections. The retrospection charms me, because I think in each I discover a partiality for me. But begone ye fallacious flattering thoughts, I must not, dare not, indulge you.

Let me hear from you, my dearest Sidney, very soon. I wish, yet dread to receive a letter from you, now you are apprized of my folly—or stile it what you please.

I am determined [trembling I write it] to abide by your advice. Use me with lenity.--Remember the unlimited authority I have given you,--- and be not too severe with

your
CAROLINE MELMOTH

LETTER VIII.

To Miss MELMOTH.

Vere-Park, July 2.

SO, you really have the conscience to suppose, you have acted a very meritorious part, in thus laying before your Sidney, the secret of your heart?——And I am to thank you for it, and to be extremely sensible of your candor, &c——I wonder what for. Did you imagine I was a stranger to that little heart? Did I not long ago tell you, your ladyship was in for it? But no. it drew up, and bridled, and blushed, I suppose.—
And

And " Lord, Sidney! In love indeed! Ridiculous!"—— You see, as very ridiculous as such a suspicion appeared to you there was some little foundation for it exclusive of that which was only to be found in my " inventive brain."

But I see nothing so mighty preposterous in your indulging hopes. To be sure there are some trifling advantages on Darnley's side. But view yourself dispassionately, and without the least self-adulation you may behold the woman worthy the picture drawn by your own hand.

In short, you must come together. I have said it, and you have made me your Fate. you are to abide by my advice. You trembled while you writ surely, you could never imagine I could differ from you in sentiments, unless when I say I think you one of the most perfect of women, which you have too much humility to allow.

I might, however, [as there was room enough,] have trifled with you, and half terrified you out of your senses, by using my full power to dissuade you from harbouring an inmate, which has gained a pretty strong footing in your breast; but I should have performed my part in a very bungling manner, and you would have discovered the cheat in every line.

You ask me, if I was ever in love? I answer, I believe not. I should despise myself, if I thought I ever was with Archer, and you would despise me perhaps, did I say I had been with Mordaunt; so I hope I may abide by my first answer.

I made my dear mother acquainted with your and Mrs Grafton's obliging invitation. She immediately, with her usual goodness, consented to grant your request, and make me happy in being with you

I think

I think her health declines that reflection makes me very unhappy. What a misfortune it would be to me to lose her! A kind, instructive, tender, parental friend have I ever found her. How perfectly resigned has she ever been to the almost tyrannical usage of a man, insensible of her worth!

I cannot always restrain my temper, when I have received any mark of my father's unworthy treatment of her. How tenderly she reproves me for the latitude of speech I run into sometimes, thro' zeal for her! —— "I complain not, my Sidney.
"Why should you? Your father has ever acted a
"father's part by you." "I wish, my dear ma-
"dam, he had acquitted himself as well in the
"duties of an husband."

"Sir William, my dear child, has many good
"qualities---He is a man of great sense. Some
"men cannot conform to common rules.—He may
"want tenderness for me, but I dare say, he will
"never be harsh to you. that would indeed make
"me unhappy."

"I can make many allowances for my husband's
"deficiency in that affection I wished to inspire
"him with. I might not perhaps be the wife of his
"choice. Our union, you have heard, my dear
"was an union of prudence an alliance of fa-
"mily rather than love but as neither of us had
"experienced that passion, our friends thought
"we had more than a chance for mutual happiness

"We cannot answer for the sentiments of our
"hearts. Perhaps Sir William could no more
"help his indifference to me, than I could loving
"him with the most fervent affection, when it
"became my duty to do so. I condemn not your
"father, Sidney, it becomes not the wife to con-
"demn her husband, much less the child to ar-
"raign the conduct of its parent."

"As

"As a proof I do not indiscriminately condemn my dear mamma, I see your behaviour in the most amiable light of uniform goodness—But why should not the marriage-state incline the man to love his wife, as a woman her husband? Surely, the vow is equally binding."

"Equally binding I allow the vow to be, Sidney. Our sex is used to subordination from its infancy. Bondage does not then sit heavy on us, as on the men. In their natures and education, they are free, unconstrained. Compulsion is ever irksome to them. Your father perhaps thought his guardians took advantage of his youth. A wife forced upon him ——— for over-persuasion is a tacit force ——— might render me displeasing to him. Duty will never sway a man, where the heart is not affected.

"For a long time I fancied I possessed the heart of my husband. From the day I yielded my hand to Sir William, by the command of my father, I sought to deserve his esteem. But bare esteem is but a weak tenure by which a a wife can keep her husband faithful. It cost me many tears and much anguish, when I was constrained from open conviction to undeceive myself. I suffered not my tears to flow before my husband, nor my anguish to burst forth in reproaches. I strove to make my home as agreeable as possible to Sir William. Sensible that my company alone was not sufficient to effect my purpose, I was never without some young companion. One of my school-fellows, of whom I was particularly fond, came to assist me in giving pleasure to my husband. I failed in my attempt, tho' she succeeded." [Here the tears fell from my dear mother's eyes.]

"But

"But what, my dearest mamma, was your friend
"unfaithful? Could my father forget his vow?"

"Spare me, my Sidney, the repetition of an
"event, which even yet gives me pain ——I was
"not born to inspire affection in the breast of the
"only man I ever loved

"Your birth seemed to excite some tenderness
"in my husband, but my long indisposition after-
"wards left him at liberty to seek amusements
"from home Four years passed, in which time
"I seldom saw him. I remained at Vere-Park.
"Sir William could very well dispense with my
"absence from London, during that time, he
"made a tour to France and Italy At his return,
"he made me a visit. My health was perfectly
"re-established —You was a lovely child ——He
"appeared charmed with you his eyes dwelt
"upon you with rapture 'Twas impossible to feel
"all the father's fondness for his infant, and not
"experience some little complacency for its mo-
"ther ——The happiest part of my life was this
"period —'Till after the birth of your dear little
"brother, I was blessed with his loved presence
"absence had not abated my affection for him

"Sir William is a man liable to be biassed, by
"his inferiors in understanding Some dissolute
"companions prevailed on him to accompany
"them on a ramble I again lost my husband I
"became habituated to his frequent emigrations.
"My happiness was now centered in my children
"My repeated anguish gave way to a calm resig-
"nation to the will of heaven, and a husband I
"could not cease to love."

My mother was never so communicative before
she used carefully to avoid entering upon this topic
Dear, worthy woman, what she has suffered!
Haughty, tyrannical even at best has my father
ever

ever been. Can I, my Caroline, be witnefs of his unworthy treatment of my amiable mother, and be filent? No, I were a brute, calmly to hear the cruel things he fometimes utters to her; for if any of his affairs go crofs, tho' through mifmanagement, fhe, poor dear foul! is fure to have his fpleen vented on her.

I faid, " I was unwilling to leave her, as fhe
" had fo little comfort, I ought not to deprive
" her of that fmall fhare I could beftow. but fhe would not hear of my refufing myfelf the pleafure and advantage fhe was fure I fhould reap in my being with you.

" You have charming fpirits, my Sidney. may
" they never be damped!---But you fhould a lit-
" tle reftrain your vivacity fometimes, as it hur-
" ries you by its impetuofity beyond the rules
" which prudence prefcribes. Mifs Melmoth
" will be a fweet example to you. her mild, her
" ———" But I won't make you vain, Caroline, as my mother's commendations of you made me. They did me honor. and I arrogated not a little to myfelf, in having fuch a dear amiable girl for my friend, the chofen companion and fharer of my heart.

When I am with you, I fhall foon difcover Sir George Darnley's paffion for you. I am fure he muft love you.

I imagine you will be in no hurry to quit the Grove.

Poor Wilton! and Louifa too! I know not whom to pity moft. I could fay a great deal about them, but have not time. Do you fuppofe a few clever things for me; you will be no lofer

My mother waits for me Adieu let me hear
soon from you In the mean time, believe me
Your faithful
SIDNEY VERE

LETTER IX

To Miss VERE

Darnley-Grove, July 5

IF your amiable mother, my dearest Sidney, is not happy, who, alas! can expect to be so? I shed tears over your letter. Ah! how worthy all the tenderness man can bestow! And yet what has her life been but one continued scene of woe? It was not a match of love. The men cannot suit their inclinations to convenience, tho' a woman oftentimes must, and your dear mamma did.

No doubt there were many men who would have been happy in an union with her. Your father alone seems insensible of her great merit.

You do not then condemn me. Ah, my Sidney! how I trembled when I opened the letter! That is, you acquiesce: but ought I to entertain any hopes? alas! can I?

Love obviates every difficulty, and, like death, puts all upon a level. but will it lessen the distance between Sir George Darnley and me?—I fear not. He is expected this afternoon —Ah! how I long to see him!

We are to go to town the beginning of next week [a pretty journey I have made of it]. As soon as possible after that, I shall expect impatiently to see my beloved Sidney do not disappoint me.

Ah!

—Ah! I cannot write any more at prefent. Sir George is juft arrived.---I muft go down.——I tremble My pulfe beats faintly How filly I am! How charming he appears advancing up to the door!——He looks up and fmiles.—Amiable, ah, too lovely Darnley!---I muft go down. Sidney adieu

Twelve. Midnight

Sure I dreamt it, or I obferved uncommon luftre in his eyes, when he approached me. He took my hand, and preffed it to his lips with warmth, I think He looked, O my God! infinitely too amiable. Who can refift him?

I feel a pleafure I was before unacquainted with, but accompanied with difquiet.

July 6th.

He intends giving a ball on Louifa's birth-day; as fhe then comes of age, Monday next the day. Many cards are difpatched to the neighbouring gentry, &c.

* * * *

Sir George talked to me a great deal this evening He defired me to keep his fecret, for that day (Monday) he intended paying his fifter her fortune, with the accumulated intereft fince his father's death How nobly generous is his behaviour!---" Young ladies," faid he, love to confi-
" der themfelves a little independent I never
" wifh my fifters to be under the leaft re-
" ftraint to me. Harriot will likewife receive
" her's. It will be a proper opportunity. Har-
" riot has great vivacity. I hope fhe will follow
" the example Louifa has ever fet her. I think
" myfelf peculiarly fortunate in both my fifters.
" Their choice of their female friends," and bowed to me, " does honor to their judgment."
He efteems me, my Sidney. He approves his
fifter's.

sister's affection for me ---Ah! may not that---But I dare not indulge the rising hope---that his esteem may in time give place to a still more tender sentiment

But when I compare his behaviour with mine, I do not find much sympathy,---which they say is the soul of love. He is free, open, collected while I now behold him with diffidence and fear I feel ever anxious to please, and at the same time seem conscious of failing in my attempt ------I revolve in my mind every word and look of the preceding day; I condemn myself every moment This I might have said, or thus I might have looked, on such or such an occasion Ah! I cease to be pleased with myself, depreciated in my own eyes, can I hope to appear amiable to an another?

But this, since I first discovered my disorder, has been, and shall invariably be my plan, I will endeavour to merit his esteem---and I need not deny it, his love, if possible and if I fail,---I must submit I must strive to bear my misfortunes with philosophy You will need a great deal, to bear with my dull epistles Adieu.

Your's ever,
CAROLINE MELMOTH.

LETTER X.

To Miss VERE

Darnley-Grove, Monday, July 10.

JUST regained my apartment, after a most delightful evening. Could it be otherwise to me when Sir George danced with me? Ah! with what joy did I receive his commendations of my performance Could I fail of acquitting myself well when led by so graceful a partner? How were all eyes fixed upon him when he began a minuet with lady

lady Amelia Stanton, a very fine woman, tall, and elegantly genteel!---But your Caroline, what words can express her feelings when he approached her, and solicited her hand for the evening?

With what inimitable grace he presented each sister with her fortune! Said the softest, the tenderest, and politest things to them, paying them at the same time, so kind, so just a compliment on their discretion And at the time he gave up all his power, offered his advice whenever they would honor him so far as to consult him his concurrence, he said, should ever go hand in hand with their choice

Louisa seemed almost overcome by his address to her, and had not a flood of tears relieved her, I really believe she would have fainted "O my " brother," sobbed the dear grateful girl, " Take, keep this loved testimony of your brother-" ly affection Where can my fortune be so se-" cure as in your hands, my brother?" Harriot very gracefully made the same tender He would by no means accept the notes, but kissing each, and folding his affectionate arms round them, he left the room In about half an hour he returned to us, with a smile upon his sweet countenance: Ah! what expression is seated there! He was exceedingly lively He took my hand, bowed on it, and leading to the harpsichord, intreated me to sing It was not in nature to refuse him, I therefore sung one suitable to the day Sir George accompanied me on the violin

I will forbear to give you a description of the dance, as it is late; and I hope soon to see, and converse with you

Wednesday, we set off for town. If you can manage to meet me there, you will add one more obligation to the many conferred on your

CAROLINE MELMOTH.

LETTER

THE HISTORY OF

LETTER XI

To Miss VERE.

Grosvenor-Square, July 14

I Sustained a disappointment in not seeing you, but a moment's reflection shewed me the absurdity of giving way to that hope, as it was morally impossible you could have had my letter till Tuesday or Wednesday But is it not too much so through life? We wish, we flatter ourselves, beyond the bounds of probability, and not till time has convinced us of the impracticability of our being gratified, are we sensible of our folly in forming such expectations

This, you will say, is no bad lesson for me True, my dear, may I profit by it!

Mrs Grafton received me with the utmost tenderness How does her every action endear her to me! best of women!

She proposes going to see the alterations at Melmoth-Castle, while you are with us, and staying there some time If she can prevail on the Darnleys, they are to accompany us thither

We had a pleasant journey to town Sir George was all life and spirits But Louisa seemed to think too much on their late guest

Lady Darnley and family are to call on us to go to Vauxhall this evening I must make some little alteration in my dress.

Sir John Evelyn called just now to pay his compliments on my arrival. I hope, nay I am sure, you will like him.

Miss Grafton is come to hasten me Adieu.

Your's eternally,
CAROLINE MELMOTH.

LETTER XII.

To Miss Vere.

Grosvenor-square, Aug. 15.

WHAT words can convey to my beloved Sidney, an idea of the pangs I endured, at our cruel and melancholy separation!——Well may it be called the death of life, for I hardly exist without you.

Can any one feel that sensibility, which is productive of pleasure and pain, in so lively a degree as your Caroline? And yet, why say I so? my kind, my sympathising Sidney's breast is actuated by the same powers as mine.

Forgive me for having written thus far without making those enquiries decency, and, permit me to say, affection, require of me.

How did you find the best of parents? How sincerely do I pity you! surely this is a proof of my love for you, since I cannot be supposed to form an idea of a child's affection to its mother, having never known a parent's care. Were I as happy as my too-presumptuous heart would wish, yet that would be an allay—Whose child am I? Am I not dependent on the bounty of strangers? Deserted in my infant years, and still left a prey to cruel uncertainty.——These reflections would make me, I say, melancholy in the happiest of situations, mine, you know, is not so.

Your absence, and the occasion of it, has left a gloom upon my spirits. I sat and wept, but found no relief from my tears.——How many real ills are there in life! Why do we then torment ourselves? But is not my attachment to Sir George Darnley become a real evil? Alas! I fear so.——

O my

O my Sidney! why did you not, on the first knowledge you had of my shewing any indication of this fatal passion, check it with all your power? But no, you soothed my flame, and, by indulging, encreased it. Why did you not use all the power I gave you? You know your influence over me. Then it might have done. In the early dawn of my distemper, your counsel might have had effect; but now it is impossible. Why did you say, you saw love in his eyes? O Sidney, your soothing flattery has undone me.

Mrs Graften has just called for me—a card from Lady Darnley to invite us to spend the evening there. Congratulate me, my Sidney, I am going to see the most lovely of men—and yet what room for congratulation?—for me, he is not lovely—cruel, heart-felt reflection!

Angels protect my friend! and grant your mother to your prayers and your
CAROLINE MELMOTH.

LETTER XIII.

To Miss MELMOTH.

Vere-park, Aug 17.

YOU will fare the better for my spirits being depressed. The Lord help me! what is the matter with the girl? Is this love that the poets paint in such glowing colours,—roses and lilies? It ought to be depicted in black,—or any thing still more dismal. I'll have none of it.

I cannot forbear my raillery, tho', my Caroline, under this affected gaiety I carry a bleeding heart. My mother, my dear indulgent mother, is, I fear, dying. The physicians attempt to flatter me me with hopes—I say attempt, for I can admit none, neither, I am sure, have they any themselves

You are melancholy, my love, I wish it was in my power to dissipate it; but how much more I stand in need of consolation, you yourself will judge, if ever you are so happy as to find a parent, and worthy of your highest reverence, as mine has ever been, and then to know and feel their loss, as I do. How very trivial is every distress, every disappointment I have hitherto sustained, opposed to this dreadful event!

The best of mothers, when she heard I was arrrived, desired to see me. " I am sorry," (said " the dear parent) my beloved Sidney, to have " broken in upon your amusements, but I could " not leave the world with that tranquillity I " ought to do, without seeing and giving you " my blessing. I feel I am not long for this life " I quit it but with one regret. Would it have " pleased heaven to have spared me 'till I had " seen you happily settled with a worthy man, " who would have guarded your tender years. " If my dearest Sidney would have given me that " satisfaction——" " O my dear mamma," I sobbed——" I mean not to reproach you, my " child; you were the best judge of your own " choice only heaven grant me my dying request " and do you, my dearest daughter, ratify it, let " your election, whenever you make one, fall on " as worthy a man as you rejected. Then shall I " I look down from the blissful regions of light " with pleasure —for I must esteem it as one of " our happiest tasks, to be permitted to behold, " and perhaps guide, thro' the slippery paths of " life, those who were most dear to us on earth"

" Be

"Be not too much afflicted at an event [we]
"are all subject to it may give offence to yo[ur]
"father. Remember all the love and duty y[ou]
"paid to me, after a few tears bestowed on m[y]
"grave, must be transmitted to him, your o[nly]
"parent left"

"If Mrs. Grafton will kindly spare her d[ear]
"Caroline, she will comfort you in your afflictio[n]
"You are at present a stranger to grief —[and]
"may you never purchase by experience so pe[r]
"fect a knowledge of it as I have done! Bu[t I]
"am going where pure delights, unallayed b[y]
"bitter reflection, will ever be my portion"

"May you, after a long series of happy year[s]
"join in those heavenly mansions the tenderest [of]
"mothers, who, if the dead have any influen[ce]
"over the living, will never cease pointing [to]
"your view the brightest and pleasantest pat[h]
"which lead to eternal felicity."

I found it was impossible to make any acknow[-]
ledgments, but by throwing myself on my knee[s]
by the bed-side, and in speechless agony sobbin[g]
over her dear cold and clammy hand. My silen[t]
grief affected her too much; in a faultering voic[e]
she bad me "retire," adding, she "would en[-]
"deavour to get a little rest."

My dear mother spoke of you again, praise[d]
and blessed you, saying, "how happy she though[t]
"herself, that she left her Sidney not without [a]
"monitress, wished you all prosperity, an[d]
"begged you would not be offended, but hope[d]
"you would mourn for her, and accept this note["]
[which I have inclosed] "for a ring, [suffer her
"not, my dearest Sidney, to be displeased with
"my request] a small legacy."

"Le[t

"Let me hope, my dearest mamma, there may not yet be any occasion for this melancholy proof of your approbation of my friend."

"Flatter not yourself, my child, there are any hopes,——I have none. All mine are now fixed above—a very few hours, and I return to my primitive clay."

Tuesday morning

I watched by my mother the whole night. She had frequent dozes, which, I hope are good symptoms, as the physicians wanted her much to have some repose. O may they prove propitious!

* * * *

One o'clock Wednesday morning

I have been begging Doctor Bertie, of whom I have a great opinion, to inform me of my mother's true state. He at first rather answered to my wishes than expectations; but on my being very urgent, saying "I was prepared, and that should the worst happen, it would be cruel in him to deceive me by false kindness," he frankly owned "nothing but a miracle could save her."—I hardly heard him out, for I sunk down wholly insensible.

My father blames me for being so ridiculously weak, as he stiles it. "Do I not think he has more reason to be afflicted, in proportion as a wife ought to be dearer than a mother?" Ought to be, I will allow him; but has he shewn he thought so? However I must conceal my distress before him. Good God! that a child must dissemble her just grief for the death of an amiable mother, for fear of giving offence to her father!

I will strive to take a little rest, having closed my eyes but for one hour—that hardly to be called sleep, since I left you.—How dreadful, not one hope left!—a servant just tells me she is in a quiet

and

and sweet sleep, unlike her former dozes. Merciful God preserve her! Who knows? the human constitution takes strange turns sometimes. It frequently happens people recover who have been given over.

Wednesday Morning, 6 o'Clock.

O Caroline, it is all over! At three I was waked. My mother was in agonies.—O my God! she expired in my arms. Why did I return to sense, and the knowledge of my miseries?

There lies the blessed saint, who was, but is no more my mother, my father, to do him justice, seems truly sensible of his loss. He weeps—but that comfort is denied me. My eyes are dry. The streams are exhausted before. O that I could shed tears! it might relieve me to weep. I feel a choaking, my heart is too big for my bosom, it hardly beats.—Wretched Sidney! lost is thy mother! ill-fated girl! But perhaps she is now benignly bending her heavenly regards on thee. I will go, and contemplate the blessed saint.

Adieu, my Caroline. write comfort to me, for at present it seems all fled—Can it ever return to your unhappy

SIDNEY VERE?

LETTER XIV.

To Miss VERE.

Grosvenor-Square, August 21.

BE not too much afflicted, my best love, with the first stroke heaven has pleased to send you. great it certainly is, it ought to be. Time's lenient hand will do much, and teach you to resign to the will of God. Death appears terrible to us, we cannot familiarize ourselves to it, although we live in daily expectation of it, either to ourselves, or friends, or acquaintance. Remember

MISS MELMOTH

Remember your dear mother's dying requeſt. I am ſorry to ſay, I fear it may diſpleaſe your father. Will he not think it a tacit reproach to him? men ill bear the ſlighteſt reproof. Yet you ſay, your father weeps. Ah! he muſt then be truly affected. Men muſt feel when they weep. You ought to pity him, my dear, he wants the nobleſt, the greateſt conſolation the human heart can receive a conſolation which, bleſſed be God! my beloved Sidney has in the moſt eminent degree—Think, my friend, how ſatisfactory are your reflections. While your eyes dwell with filial fondneſs on the remains of your parent, how great, how conſolatory your feelings, the conſciouſneſs of never having given that dear parent uneaſineſs, on the contrary, contributing all in your power to make her happy—Now ſhe is completely ſo. Ah! do not, by your lamentations, give room for belief you wiſh the dear departed again to return to a world not worthy of her.

I was almoſt afraid to requeſt my dear benefactreſs permiſſion to leave her for a little time, to endeavour to mitigate your grief by participating it, but ſhe, ever preventing my wiſhes, "Would " it not, my Caroline, be charity to go to your " friend in diſtreſs now?" "If, my deareſt ma-" dam, you will add to your former indulgences, " a few weeks to my Sidney, it would only be " increaſing the weight of an obligation, which it " will never be in my power otherwiſe than by " grateful thanks to repay."

" No acknowledgments, my deareſt love; the " pleaſure I have found in your company, more " than outweighs thoſe obligations you mention, " you are my deareſt treaſure, left by the beſt of " brothers." I ſnatched her hand, and fervently kiſſing it——" May that heaven you imitate, re-
" pay

" pay your unspeakable goodness!" Tears of benevolence filled her eyes and she clasped me to her bosom, while mine ran over with grateful transport

Sure, my Sidney, she is more than woman!

I think, had I a mother, I could not feel more reverential affection for her than I do for Mrs Grafton,—or indeed, could I have more cause? To my natural parents, whoever they were, 'tis true I am indebted for my existence, but that was only making me sensible of misery, from which they sought not to rescue me. What would have become of me, had not the ever-respected Mrs. Melmoth taken the poor forlorn infant? Mr Grafton too followed her noble brother's pious example, in succouring helpless innocence

Heaven, which deprived me of my parents, bestowed these invaluable friends on me in my tenderest years, and, when reason began to dawn, gave me my Sidney Vere O then ought I to complain? Chide me, my love, when I so far forget myself

The testimony your amiable mother left me of her love, I receive as you desire me The smallest token would have been sufficient She gave me her Sidney, had I more to ask?

The Darnley family, whither we were going when I wrote last, inquired most kindly after you the mild Louisa shed a tear for the distress of my friend

I say nothing about that visit there were many people there, too many to be agreeable

Miss Grafton has again this evening talked of you I ventured to hint the necessity of your having somebody with you " You shall be with
" her, my love, as soon as you please, only do
" not forget how happy I shall be to see you again"

On

On Monday next I propose setting out for Vere Park, on Tuesday I hope to embrace my beloved Sidney, who is so deservedly dear to her
faithful
CAROLINE MELMOTH.

LETTER XV

To Miss VERE

Grosvenor-Square, October 5.

HERE I am, safe arrived, after a journey with a heavy heart, occasioned by parting with my friend, which, however, grew proportionably lighter as it approached Mrs Grafton's.

Tender, and truly affectionate, was that dear lady's reception of me. How many flattering compliments did she pay me on my improvements by the healthful air of the country!

But before I go any farther, let me thank you and yours, for the polite favors I received while happy with you.

I hope your father will still continue that kindness he professes for you now. Be it your task, my dear, to conciliate his affection, you will then, I pronounce, be a happy girl.

You will have a very agreeable neighbour in lady Betty Crauford. She is a sensible woman, and perfectly amiable in her disposition and person. I have seen her once. Mrs Cleveland, who is her intimate friend, gives her a high character. She has every qualification to render the marriage-state completely happy—A news-paper phrase that—

October 6.

This morning the Miss Darnleys called on me, to congratulate me, or themselves rather, they said, on my arrival in town. Louisa asked Mrs Grafton.

ton "if she could spare her child to go to visit her
"other mamma, who longed to see her." Mr
Grafton kindly replied, "She loved me too we
"to deprive me of any pleasure, but added, yo
"must expect to see me in the afternoon, wit
"Letty, consider we have had but little of our
"Caroline's company."

I was preparing to make some little alteratio
in my dress, but they prevented me, Harriot sa,
ing, "I should do mischief enough. For her part
"she was heartily glad her swains were out o
"town."

Lady Darnley received me with open arm,
and said many kind things to me in her polite
easy way

Do you say nothing of the Baronet, Caroline
Ah, my Sidney! did you suppose I should forge
him?---Shall I tell you how my heart fluttered
when I heard his voice, how I trembled when
he approached me, and how silly I looked and
answered his compliments? To what purpose? It
you have ever been in love, it will be needless,
if you know nothing of that passion, still more so

But yet I must say how much I was flattered
by the united praises of the whole family they
all profess to admire me. Why cannot I be content with the esteem of the first of men? O that
I could!

He looks sometimes, Sidney, as if —— but I
dare not indulge myself. Ah, how happy should
I be, if those looks came from the heart!

Adieu, my dearest Sidney I suppose you have
paid your visit to Lady Betty pray tell me in
your next, how you like her

Your's for ever,
CAROLINE MELMOTH

LETTER XVI.

To Miss Melmoth.

Vere-park, Oct. 12.

LADY Betty Crauford answers the newspaper-phrase most emphatically. her perfections do honor to your judgment, in giving her a character so justly her due.

I believe she is not in general thought handsome by the Men, though I have seen many who have been reigning toasts not half so pleasing, nor have possessed half her personal charms in my eyes — There is an open sincerity in her countenance, which plainly indicates a noble heart; my acquaintance, you know, has been short, and yet I have received proofs of her candor.

When I paid my first visit to Crauford-Manor, which was the day after they appeared at church, I was vastly pleased with her ladyship's manner and address, though I thought I perceived a kind and reserve hang on her brow; but I attributed it to the natural disposition of the English towards strangers — I made my visit rather an unfashionable one, at least it would have appeared so to many London Belles, but as we became more acquainted, I found such pleasure in her conversation, that I had no inclination to quit that, for a dull tête-à-tête at home — All civility and affection seemingly has flown away since your departure — gloomy reserve takes place —

Crauford, in his usual good-natured way, begged we might be very intimate, for said he, " I " have taken my Betty from an exceeding agree- " able family, which I am certain she will not " feel the loss of, if you will, when you can, " oblige us with your company."

In two days Lady Betty returned my visit quite in a sociable way. When we had been chatting a good while on indifferent things—if any subject can be termed so, on which she expatiates with the utmost propriety—she said, "I fancy, Miss Vere, your first prepossessions were not much in my favor"—"On the contrary," answered I, "I never beheld a person whom I was so desirous of pleasing at first sight as your ladyship; nor do I very well understand your meaning, since I am conscious"—"I beg your pardon for interrupting you," said her ladyship, "I assure you I meant to condemn myself, for I must own—you will forgive me, I dare hope, as my sentiments now are very different—notwithstanding the high character Mr. Crauford gave of you, I yet felt some little prejudices which I am afraid appeared too plain on my countenance, as it ever corresponds with my heart but I had been a very short time in your company ere they vanished, and left in their room a growing esteem, which I am sure will increase with my further knowledge of you— I have long known you by name—Nor will you wonder at my conceiving some little distaste to a lady (for that was really the case,) who had rendered a near, dear, and worthy relation of mine unhappy."

"I have listened with great impatience to your ladyship; but for heaven's sake make me easy by an explanation."

"You had once a lover"———.

"I have had many But none as I know of who deserve these epithets, much less who could boast a relationship to your family."

"The gentleman I mean, needed not to boast a consanguinity which could not add to his me-
"rit

"rit—I mean Mr. Mordaunt."—" Mr. Mordaunt! he your relation?"—and will you credit me, Caroline, I felt myself change color, and all in a tremor—Conscious error—I suppose.

"Yes, my dear Miss Vere, Mr Mordaunt is my relation; but much nearer allied to me by the ties of affection than those of blood I was his confidante, and acquainted with his ardent passion for you, freely and intirely: but as I was not apprized of the reason of its going off, I could not help imagining there must be some error on the lady's side, who could oblige a man of his known sense and honor to leave his native country, and, I much fear, his happiness. He has been lost to all his friends since the unhappy failure of his wishes And though a more than common friendship subsisted between us, he has never corresponded with me since his departure, which his despair suggested to him, as the only means of restoring the peace of mind he had lost.

"O Miss Vere, you missed in him a man, whose only study would have been your felicity, yet if your heart owned a prepossession in favor of another, you are to be justified"

Ah Caroline! was not this a cutting reproof? I was greatly affected—Tears stood in my eyes; Lady Betty wiped her's

"And can you yet behold me with any degree of regard? no, rather you must despise me.——
"And yet, my dear Lady Betty, were you acquainted with every circumstance, perhaps you would not so much condemn me"

"I do not, why should I, when my cousin has intirely acquitted you? his last letter was filled with encomiums of her, whom he said he must endeavour to think of no more. hard task for one who loved so well!—Ah! how "unhappy

"unhappy was he to place his affections on the only woman who was not sensible of his merit!"

"I must take shame to myself. I was sensible he had great merit but what impression does the merit of a man make in general on a giddy girl of sixteen? I esteemed him; but I felt not that warmth I expected was to fill my breast Just come from a boarding-school, I imagined all mankind were to be my slaves, and a few frothy speeches, such as I had read in Clelia or Cassandra, from the lips of an officer, sunk deeper in my mind, than the genuine worth of Mr Mordaunt The one, from a consciousness I suppose of his own demerit, studied by flattery to engage my good opinion of myself, as the means of ingratiating himself in my favor, the other strove to make himself agreeable to a woman of sense, and unhappily thought I was one. He was recommended by my parents, and endeavoured to conciliate their esteem by his generous principles of honor, but in the romances I had read, there was no precedent for such proceedings

"I had been flattered into a belief of beauty by Captain Archer Mr Mordaunt, from mistake, paid his court to the perfections of mind he fancied I possessed Which, with a girl under the influence of folly and vanity, were most likely to succeed? I could treat Archer as I pleased, still with the most obsequious servility would he support my tyranny but it was not so with Mr Mordaunt, he had a proper knowledge of his own merit, and what he deserved

"On some gross affront put upon him by Archer, which his good sense suggested to him was occasioned by my partiality for that wretch

"—he

"—he challenged him.—They fought——you
"know the confequences; and tho' they did not
"prove fo fatal as might have been, you loft a
"relation, and I——what I deferved

"I hear he is married I am glad of it, and
"fincerely hope he meets with that felicity he
"had reafon to expect, in the poffeffion of a
"woman who loves him that felicity he could
"never have found in me

"His affection gave as many charms to my
"mind, as the hopes of my fortune made Archer
"beftow on my perfon But although their mo-
"tives were different, I had certainly no right to
"either"

"O Mifs Vere," faid Lady Betty, taking my
hand,—"I muft ever regret your not being my
"relation. How happy would Mordaunt have
"been with you! it is not your humility can
"eclipfe your many perfections You ftrive to
"derogate from your own merit; but every word
"you utter endears you to me Grant me your
"efteem, or I fhall be very unhappy in knowing
"you, only to lament I have not worth to engage
"it"

"If, my dear Lady Betty, you do not defpife
"me, I fhall be content, leave it to my endea-
"vours and affiduity, to deferve more from you."

"Amiable creature!" fhe called me—"But I
"muft leave you, my charming Mifs Vere. May
"you, whenever you place your affections, meet
"with fuch a man as Mordaunt!" I fighed——
"I dare not fubfcribe to your wifh But I made
"a refolution, and hitherto have kept it, never
"to give my hand, much lefs encourage any man
"inferior to that gentleman in merit"

"O where was that noble heart buried?"
exclaimed Lady Betty, embracing me; "but I
"muft

"must leave you Let me see you often; adieu"
And away she tripped, leaving me, I own, rather
in the humdrums—He is married—Well, I never loved him, tho' I felt an esteem for him, I
have never experienced since for any man. But I
will say no more upon this subject I shall be very
often at lady Betty's. Home is not as it used to
be.

My Kitty is going to leave me It is for her
advantage, I hope. you know she was going to be
married. I shall want a servant in her place; she
says she will not quit my service till I am suited,
but I shall not incommode her, to avoid a small
inconvenience to myself

I hope you have not forgot the promise you made
me of your picture hasten Meyers with it; I
want it much it will serve to sooth me, when
you are absent from

Your

SIDNEY VERE.

LETTER XVII.

TO MISS VERE.

Grosvenor-Square, October 20

I Am happy you are pleased with lady Betty,
whom I think an amiable woman

The picture, my dear, I at last send you, the
delay was occasioned by an accident Ah! that accident has given further encouragement to a too
presumptuous hope

One evening, the beginning of last week, there
was a large party at lady Darnley's One room
was filled with card-tables Many of us young
folks were assembled in another Cards were utterly disclaimed Well what should we do to divert
ourselve-

ourselves? We had severally played on the harpsicord. Harriot in a jesting way said, "Well, good "people, what shall we do? Suppose we play at "draw-gloves, questions and commands, or judge-"advocate." Simple as the proposition was, it was closed with immediately by the gentlemen.—
"For then," said one, "we shall have forfeits."

Sir George was deputed interrogatist. He asked us a number of droll questions, some he put to me, I was scarcely capable of answering. The commands were as usual. A great many forfeits I was, thro' inattention, obliged to pay. After delivering a smelling-bottle, pocket-book, &c. I took out the shagreen case, wherein was my picture, which a servant had brought from Meyers, and gave to me just before I came out.

Sir George collected the forfeits, which were to be redeemed. It lasted a long time, and we were heartily fatigued by this childish play. The proposal of the forfeits being returned, was at length agreed to, and they were accordingly delivered. Sir George forgot to give me the picture; indeed I did not think of reminding him. I was sorry for it when I came home, as I had intended immediately to send it you.

Two days after he called upon us. I then reminded him he had not given me the case. He made a thousand apologies for his negligence, saying "he had put it in his waistcoat-pocket, and "never thought of it afterwards, as he had not "worn those cloaths since, but he would take the "first opportunity of returning it. But is it your "picture, Miss Melmoth?"—"Yes, Sir"—
"Ladies seldom have their pictures drawn for their "own pocket," said he, looking as I thought tenderly inquisitive at me——" That was drawn at
"the

"the desire of a particular friend, Sir George"
"Male or female?" he smilingly asked "Fe
"male, Sir; for Miss Vere"——"I am very
"glad to hear it is a female particular friend I
"own I was apprehensive it had been for some
"happy distinguished lover"

"I thought, Sir George,"————and I look
ed a little archly,——"it had remained in your
"waistcoat-pocket, and that you were a stranger
"to the contents of the case"——A blush over
spread his face, he hesitated "A— why—I
"—did---just look at it, but it quite slipped my
"memory, faith. I wonder how I could be so
"forgetful But you shall have it Apropos,
"lord F—— declares he never heard a voice
"equal to yours, you know you were command-
"ed to sing How was it? "Tho' his passion in
"silence the youth would conceal"----Do my
"charming Miss 'Melmoth, favor me with a
"repetition of that sweet song" "Excuse me,
"Sir George---I am not now commanded"——
"No, you were not born to be commanded, but
"to command over all mankind" I am deceived,
or a half-smothered sigh accompanied these words
—He took my hand, gently pressing it "Permit
"me to lead you to the harpsicord" Tho' the
pressure was very gentle, it caused so much palpitation in my heart, I knew not how to conceal it

Miss Grafton at that instant joined us. "To in-
"force my intreaties, is the lovely Miss Grafton
"come," said he "Do join in a duet with
"Caroline?" "No, no," smiling "she does
"not want a foil" "Nor you a compliment, my
"dear," I rejoined ---"But will you favour me
"with your assistance?" After a few tender speeches from Sir George, she consented, and we performed "La baronesse amibile" pretty tolerably I
though

thought I could have done much better had my dear Marquis joined his Cecchina

Yesterday we were in St James's-square A-gain say you? Aye, again and again, my dear; we are but as one family

I hinted to Sir George, he had " a pretty waist- "coat on, and I believed was the same I had the "pleasure of seeing him in before"

" I understand you, my dear Miss Melmoth," bowing, " you are very desirous of depriving me " of a great pleasure; I have it not in my pocket " at present the next time I see you I will re- " turn your lovely picture"

This afternoon he brought it to me, and put- ting it in my hand, made a polite compliment to me, tender too I thought, for I felt it thro' every nerve—Ah! how sweetly he looked! How grace- ful is his every action!

His sisters are continually repeating his praise before me

Ah! why do they? It is not that they wish I should behold their brother with partial eyes. ah! no. I should incur their heaviest displeasure were they to suspect the feelings of my heart

I am constrained to keep a constant guard over my looks and words, especially before Louisa. love has given her searching eyes

I have been contemplating—I am almost ashamed to say what—but my miniature, I opened the case, and, involuntarily sighing, fixed my eyes upon the resemblance of your simple friend · per- haps said I to myself——I have not yet learned to think aloud—the finest eyes in the world have been thus employed a train of thoughts crowded in my imagination; I pressed the inanimate crystal to my lips—because may be Sir George had done the

same

same A silent tear stole down my cheek—becau[se]
—but I blush to repeat my follies. Do you pa[r]
don them however in

>   Your faithful and
>   unalterable friend,
>   CAROLINE MELMOTH

LETTER XVIII.

To Miss MELMOTH

Vere-Park, October 19

I HAVE just met with an adventure, which I
sit down to communicate to my lovely Caroline, without further preface

This morning, being rather melancholy for want
of a companion—lady Betty Crauford being absent—my recent loss of the best of mothers ever in
my mind, I rambled over the fields adjoining, to
the extremity of the park, when finding myself
fatigued, and perceiving a little cottage at a small
distance, I made up to it A decent-looking old
woman was at the door I asked her leave to rest
myself a few minutes in her porch, she made me
many aukward compliments in our country dialect,
and gave me a very hearty invitation to her house
and fare

"She told me, if I would be pleased to walk in-
"to her humble parlour; there was a young wo-
"man, much more fitting to converse with my
"ladyship than she a poor silly woman was" I
asked her a few questions about the young woman
she spoke of? She answered, "she had lodged
"with her about five or six weeks; that she be-
"lieved she was poor, and would be glad to wait
"on

" on some lady, if she could hear of any one that
" wanted a servant."

As the good woman had made me an offer of her parlour, I desired her to shew me into it, saying " I should be glad to see the person she mentioned, as I might be of service to her,—being " at present myself in want of a servant."

My hostess ushered me into a clean red-bricked room, where was sitting at work a young woman, neatly, tho' plainly dressed, seemingly about my age. She rose. I made an apology for interrupting her, begged I might not disturb her,—for she seemed as if she intended to leave the room,—adding, " unless she gave me her company, I could " not think of obliging her to leave a place " where she was amusing herself, but would, after " asking her pardon for my intrusion, leave her " at liberty to pursue her employment, and return " with the good woman of the house to the porch." ——She spoke in very polite terms, and further said, " she should be very happy in the honor of " my conversation for a little while, as she had " not always been used"—a sigh at these words stole from her—" to the company of people she " was now with, tho' perhaps it had been better " for her if she had, as then she possibly might " have escaped the mortification of knowing how " seldom sincerity was found among people of an-
" other rank."

I don't-know-how, I felt myself rather interested in this young person; I was going to express myself to that purpose when my kind hostess came into the room. " It is the luckiest accident in the " world," said she, addressing herself to her lodger, " I dare say her ladyship's honor can tell you of " a place." Her abrupt manner made the poor young creature blush; but totally regardless of the

pain

pa n she put her to, on she went—" To be sure,
" there must be many places that would suit you
" it must not be of much labor to be sure, for
" certain, because as why, you are not fitting for
" much houshold work, but to wait on such a
" young gentlewoman as her ladyship's honor God
" bless her!" with a court'sy —I endeavoured to
stop this old woman's loquacity, and said " She
" must be mistaken as to the gentlewoman, how
" ever, she was very obliging, and it she would
" give me leave to have a little private conversati-
" on with the young lady, I should take it as a fa
" vor "——After a few more wife sentences, away
the old houswife trotted, and left us to ourselves
" I cannot suppose, madam," said I, " you are in
" the distress the good woman who has just left us
" seemed to signify I was sorry to find she was
" so abrupt"

" Indeed, madam," said she, " there is great
" truth in what she said, and however I appeared
" shocked, I am yet greatly obliged to her for her
" zeal in attempting to serve me If I could be
" recommended to any place, I should be very
" happy, but I am so little known here, that I
" despair of hearing of any thing to suit me."

" I have," said I, " just parted with a servant
But I can never suppose, you were born to any
servile employ"

" Many, madam, who have had far better ex-
" pectations in life than myself, have been obli-
" ged to submit to such things I should ima-
" gine there could be nothing, in waiting on
" a young lady, which I cannot perform with
" ease: and I should look on this day as the hap-
" piest of my life, if it was to introduce me to
" your service."

" That, madam, I cannot think of for tho' I
" require very little attendance from a servant,
" yet I should not know how to give the most gen-
" the

" tle commands to a perfon, perhaps as well born
" as myfelf but if I can make my propofal agree-
' ible to my father, I will take an opportunity of
" feeing or fending to you to-morrow."

She thanked me in a polite manner. When finding myfelf fufficiently refted, and gratifying my hoftefs, I walked home.

After dinner, I acquainted my father with the adventure, and mentioned my propofal of taking her in the room of Kitty. "And who pray"—in his ufual fweet way of fpeaking to my poor mother——" is to recommend her? How do you
" know what or who fhe is? I have no notion of
" thefe fudden attachments, the refult of roman-
" tic ideas inculcated by thofe who fhould have
" taken pains to have inftilled into you different
" fentiments. The firft thing fhe does, I fuppofe,
" will be to introduce fome of her fellows here,
" who may give rife to another adventure; your
" foolifh fex think of nothing elfe but I will not
" have my houfe made the fcene of action."

" I muft have a fervant, Sir, faid I, therefore
" may as well try her. I am fure, Sir, you have
" never had any reafon to believe your daughter,
" was fond of adventure you might have fpared
" your general farcafm on the fex, among whom,
" I dare fay, you made as many fools as you found.
" But altho' this young creature is not perfectly
" known, muft we conclude her a bad one? fure-
" ly that is judging very hard."——"Well, well
" do as you will I defire not to interfere." And fo, Caroline, I intend to do, if I can.

My father knows my fpirits are depreffed with nothing but harfh reflections on my dear mother's memory. he therefore takes pleafure, whenever he can, to throw out hints to her difadvantage, never blaming me, but obliquely glancing at the faults of the mother inherited by the child: but how vain,
how

how impotent his defign! do not thofe inuendoes
raife her noble character? They do, and I revere
her more, if poffible, every time he fpeaks difrefpectfully of her, from the confcioufnefs of her
fuperior worth, who, all angel as fhe was, could
yet do her duty, with chearfulnefs and inclination,
to a man much her inferior

I fhall now take my leave, dear Caroline, as
my eyes are almoft clofed Pleafant dreams to my
charming friend!

October 20

In confequence of my refolution, I went to the
farm to-day, where I was immediately introduced
to the old woman's lodger, who, as fhe did not
appear fo melancholy as the preceding day, looked,
I thought, very pretty. She received me with
great joy, feemingly mingled with doubt I made
hafte to inform her, " I was refolved to take her
" home with me, and that I fhould look upon her
" as my companion, 'till fhe gave me caufe by
" mifbehaviour to alter my conduct, which, however, I could not think would ever be the cafe
" but as fhe was an intire ftranger to me, and every
" body in this part of the country, I fhould be
" glad to be acquainted with her motive for com-
" ing hither"

" I owe you, madam," faid fhe, " every thing,
" and if you will grant me patience, I will endeavour
" to recollect every circumftance of my paft mi-
" fery It will undoubtedly give me pain, but
" the pleafure I fhall feel in obliging you, will in
" fome meafure compenfate the anguifh I muft
" neceffarily experience in the recital

" I do not doubt but you will find much in my
" unhappy ftory to blame me for I muft there-
" fore befpeak your partial ear, while I relate my
" woes

" My

MISS MELMOTH

"My real name, madam, is Arnold. I was born in Gloucestershire, my father is a clothier there. I have many brothers and sisters, but I know not how, I was by much the favorite. I dare not think it was owing to any superior merit which my parents discovered in me; had that been the cause of their partiality, I had not now been here.

"About a year since, there was a regiment of of soldiers quartered in our town. Their company enlivens every place. The officers in general behaved extremely well, for which they were taken notice of, and invited into the genteel families in the neighbourhood.

"Among the rest who frequented our house, was Captain Clayton, a young man, who, by his good sense and specious appearance, gained the esteem of every one.

"He soon found out I was agreeable, at least he took all opportunities of making me think he did, and it had the desired effect; for when I began to sound my heart, it told me Captain Clayton was the most agreeable of men.

"I must inform you, madam, before I became acquainted with the Captain, there was a person with whom my father had dealings, who had for some time paid his addresses to me, which I accepted, not from any attachment I had to the man,—he being many years older than myself, but from a childish desire of appearing superior at our assemblies to all my young companions. I received Mr Barker as other girls do their lovers, whom they have no further inclination for than the gratifying their vanity for dress and show, my then chief foible. I have said he was older than myself, but he was rich, and had he been the age of Methuselah, I should have made no
objections

"objections to him before I had seen Captain Clay
"ton

"My new lover soon found he had a rival, tho
"he was master of too much penetration to ima
"gine he was a favorite one However, to gain
"a perfect knowledge of my sentiments, he pre
"tended to believe I was not at all averse to an
"union with Mr Barker, and took many occasions
"of saying how happy a man Mr Barker was,
"how much he was to be envied!---Not so much
"perhaps, said I to him one day, if his felici
"depends on my attachment to him It is a match
"intirely proposed by my father"--"By your fa
"ther! said he, with the utmost surprise What,
"can a father sacrifice a child to such a wretch
"nature, nor laws human or divine, can give
"sanction to such barbarity The ecstatic joy I
"feel at hearing you do not love him, can hardly
"make amends for the knowledge I now have of
"your father's intentions

"He urged a thousand things to prove his as
"sertion, that a father can have no right to guide
"or restrain the children's affection; that love
"was free, nor would be controlled——In short,
"madam, he was not long making me a convert to
"his doctrine a doctrine which my heart had
"long suggested to me, and the consequences
"were, I was more and more in love with Capt
"Clayton; and all the tendernesses which my
"father and mother had heaped upon me from
"my birth, were cancelled in my mind, by their
"horrid proposition of my marrying a man, so
"totally unworthy possessing so valuable a trea-
"sure, as the Captain's elaborate professions of
"adoration had made me fancy myself.

"From that moment as my passion for Captain
"Clayton encreased, a settled aversion filled my
"breast

"breast for Mr Barker, not could I behold my
"parents without some indignation.

"Mr. Barker now became very pressing to have
"this business, which had long been in hand,
"brought to a conclusion. I framed twenty ex-
"cuses, but neither he or my father would hear
"of any. I imagine they began to suspect my
"attachment to Captain Clayton, for upon a tri
"fling dispute between them one evening, my fa-
"ther forbad him the house. I was present at the
"quarrel, words had run very high, I thought I
"should have expired at the sound but my fear
"of discovering the real state of my mind I believe
"kept me from fainting. What a night did I
"pass! the most terrifying ideas harrowed up my
"soul. My lover departing in anger on one hand,
"and not the least hope remaining of my escaping
"the impending danger of marrying a man
"detested on the other, prevented my sleeping

"The next day my father, with a sternness un-
"usual to him, told me he would grant no more
"delays, and that I should be kept a close prison-
"er, if I did not immediately consent to per-
"form my engagements. I wept,---begged, and
"intreated in vain. The odious Barker too came,
"with his horrid solicitations that I would bless
"him. my mother was deaf to my pleading,
"and my brother and sisters took an ill-natured
"pleasure---because I had been the favorite---in
"the misery they saw me undergo.

"My father, with a look and voice which
"made me tremble, again asked me, if I would
"chearfully give my hand to Mr Barker.------I
"threw myself at his feet, and, almost suffocated
"by tears and sobs, in a tone scarce articulate, I
"I implored his pity, in such a manner as would
"have

" have melted the heart of a tyrant: but it h
" no effect on any present
" Girl, said my father, taking both my clasp
" hands as they were held up, in one of his, a
" presently dashing them from him—I know
" whom this disobedience is owing, but m
" everlasting curses be my portion, as they sh
" be your's, if I do not make you comply wi
" my wishes! Go to your chamber, never sh
" you come out of it but to go to church wi
" the man I have chose for you —What more h
" might add I know not, for by this time I w
" insensible of any afflictions When I came
" little to myself, a maid-servant led me up to n
" chamber I threw myself drowned in tea
" upon the bed I lamented aloud my cruel fate
" and called upon death to ease my sufferings

" Happy had it been for me, had I then know
" a period to my life! Alas! what did I then fee
" to what I have since experienced! Ah my God
" those were days of felicity to what I have sinc
" seen and yet I am living!

" Grief so violent was not possible to hav
" long continuance, especially in a girl of m
" natural life and spirit In a few hours I became
" capable of reasoning with some degree of calm-
" ness which however I was unable to attain
" till I had in my own mind determined to un
" dergo all kinds of severity rather than give m
" hand to Mr Barker; who now appeared in so
" odious a light, that my soul recoiled at the bare
" reflection of him

" I now rose from the bed which had been the
" scene of meditation, and walked gloomily about
" my prison The maid, whom I looked on as
" my jaileress, brought me something for dinner
" I could not forbear venting some of my spleen
" on

on her, which I did in pretty rough terms;
however I had the prudence to recollect myself,
reflecting it would be better if possible to gain
one friend, than to add her to my enemies. I
made her some apologies for my harshness, and
told her she might leave what she had got, and
presently I would try to eat.

"In the evening the maid again came into the
room, and asked me for my keys.—For what?
said I—I am ordered, miss, to take your pens
and ink from you, as my master is apprehensive you will contrive to write to Captain Clayton: and you may be sure he will take all precaution to hinder your corresponding with the
captain, till he leaves the town, or you are
married.—Mention not the horrid sounds, I
exclaimed, I'll die, starve—rot on a dunghill,
first——Such, most likely, will be your fate,
miss, for my master just now swore you should
not live, unless you married Mr Barker——
Leave the room, said I,——I cannot bear your
presence; it is hateful to me——Upon my
word, miss, you are vastly hurt, certainly, to
be forced to marry a man so many would be
glad to have in their power——Saying which,
away she went grumbling she would tell my
father of my treatment, &c.

"I was by this time so deprived of all recollection, that my determination of endeavouring
to gain her to my party never recurred to me.
I stamped about the room like one totally out of
their senses. My tears, which now began to
flow plentifully, relieved my aking heart a little.
However I spent my night pretty much like the
former.

"The next day I sat by a window which looked
into a back lane, there was no other on that side
"the

"the houſe except one in the parlour beneath
"which was conſtantly ſhut As I was looking
"out of the window, I obſerved a beggar-man
"who walked backwards and forwards very often
"and frequently looked up I beheld him with
"attention, nor could I help envying him, who
"I ſuppoſed might do as he pleaſed, go where he
"would, and enjoy the bounty of well-diſpoſed
"perſons, with ſome one whom he had choſe
"out for his partner While ſuch cogitations poſ-
"ſeſſed my mind, I perceived, in gazing up-
"my window, he made a kind of ſign I not
"all gueſſing the meaning of the mendicant, made
"a motion with my hand, upon which he look-
"ed up earneſtly, and ſmiled, at the ſame time
"putting aſide his old ragged coat, diſcovered
"my view the uniform of Captain Clayton I
"immediately found the pretended beggar was m
"dear lover Nothing I think could equal my
"joy on this occaſion it appeared ſuch an inde-
"lible proof of the ſincerity of his love, that I
"was almoſt glad of the opportunity that had
"given me a knowledge of it.——I made him
"underſtand by ſigns, how happy I was to ſee
"him which however I was not contented with,
"yet how to let him know more, puzzled me a
"long time But a woman's invention, moſt fer-
"tile in exigences, ſoon pointed out the only me-
"thod Pencil, pen, ink, and paper, were taken
"from me Notwithſtanding all theſe neceſſary
"implements were unpoſſeſſed by me, I ſpeedily
"ſupplied all deficiencies thus, I took the lead out
"of the ſleeve of a gown, which, with a knife, I
"made by cutting——attended by ſome difficulty
"tho'——into a kind of ſubſtitute for a better pen-
"cil this firſt accompliſhed, ſomething to write
"on was to be next conſidered, this I remedied
"by

"by tearing out the blank leaf of a book thus
" was I completely furnished for a scribe, when
" a thought which I had not meditated on before,
" occurred to me,——to what purpose should I
" write? I could throw my billet out of the win-
" dow, but could I follow it? If I could, would the
" captain receive me as readily? But these reflec-
" tions did not last long I had surmounted the
" preceding difficulties, and every other vanished
" at one glance my lover gave me

" Well, I wrote my note, wherein, in a few
" words, I told him of my father's resolution of
" keeping me prisoner 'till I would consent to the
" hated marriage, but I would die first

" I begged him to believe his image was too
" firmly rooted in my heart, for any severity to
" eradicate it, and concluded, if he continued
" in the same sentiments he professed in happier
" days, I should hope to receive an answer to
" this, which he might convey by means of a
" string I would contrive to hang out of the win-
" dow at night

" I folded up part of the remaining lead in the
" note, and gently lifting up the window a little
" way, for fear of making a noise, I threw it
" hastily down to my captain, who stooping down
" quick picked it up, kissed it, and putting it in
" his bosom, went with all expedition away, left
" by loitering there any longer, he might subject
" himself to the suspicion of any of the family

" With what impatience did I wait for even-
" ing, when the duskiness would favor my design
" of lowering the string which was to bring me
" the only cordial to my drooping spirits, I had
" received since my confinement ——except the
" first discovering him under the disguise of a
" beggar

         " I took

"I took a ball of knotting which fortunately I
"had in my room, to which I fixed a small
"work-bag, and in that put the fellow-piece of
"lead to that which had enabled me to write,
"that I might more easily let it down, which I
"did the moment I could hazard it with any se
"curity

"I heard somebody cough gently, and could
"with difficulty discern a man who I doubted
"not was the person I wanted I found by the
"dragging of the string he had accomplished our
"purpose, and with great precipitation, attended
"with caution, I drew it in

"Joyful was I when I perceived a large letter,
"which however I could not read, by reason I
"had not light enough to see the words, my
"father, in order to be more rigorous, having
"forbad me the use of candle My impatience
"to peruse this dear testimony of Captain Clay
"ton's love, you may believe, madam, was very
"violent · however there was no remedy but pa
"tience, and I was constrained to wait till morn-
"ing, before I could give myself that satisfaction

"It gave me infinite pleasure——as I drew
"happy conclusions from it——that my lover
"had the precaution to supply me [knowing my
"inability] with two pens, a few sheets of paper,
"and a little phial of ink, inestimable treasures
"to me!

"When morning light appeared sufficient to
"allow me to gratify my desire of seeing what my
"lover would do to save me from misery, I
"took the dear letter, which, as well as the rest
"of the contents of the work-bag, had been my
"bed-fellow, and eagerly kissing it, prepared to
"regale myself with the contents"

Do you not wonder, my dear Caroline, that I can remember so much of Miss Arnold's history? I committed it to paper on my coming home——and am now only transcribing

As the post is going out, I will send what I have written

I really find myself greatly interested in her distresses I dare say you would like her. I am certain you would, for are not your sentiments the same, at least you flatter me they are the same, with those of
Your ever faithful
SIDNEY VERE.

LETTER XIX.

To Miss MELMOTH

Vere-Park, October 21.

I Proceed in Miss Arnold's words:
" Captain Clayton's letter was filled with
" the most ardent professions of unabating affecti-
" on He urged, he conjured me to fly with him·
" we might concert some scheme very easily for
" my escape, and, if I loved like him, that love
" would excite me to undertake any difficulty to
" put myself under his protection that he would
' guard me with his life 'till he could reach Scot-
" land, where he would make me his by the most
" indissoluble ties——Expatiated at large on the
" happiness attending an union of those whom love
" had paired, saying much more than was necef-
" sary at that time to convince me, that to meet
" my felicity, I could find it no where but in his
" arms. He opposed to the blissful scene he had
" just been drawing, the dreadful contrast I must
" experience

"experience if I confented to my ruin,——'or
" no better title could he afford my marriage with
" Mr Barker

" What could I do? I debated fome time, whe-
" ther I had better follow the dictates of my love
" than my duty It would be affectation as well
" as an untruth, was I to fay the conflict lafted
" any very long time At firft, I had fome fcru-
" ples of confcience, which fuggefted whether a
" parent's not fulfilling their duty could abfolve a
" child in difobedience but a fecond perufal of
" my epiftle granted me as abfolute a difpenfation
" as ever the Pope did any one Therefore, I
" delayed not writing immediately, for fear of a
" furprife, to acquaint my lover, (as he informed
" me, he would come very early under the win-
" dow, difguifed as before) that I had come to the
" refolution to truft myfelf with him, and as I
" placed fo much dependance on his honor, I
" fhould receive that as a guarantee, that he would
" never give me caufe to repent my fo eafily con-
" fenting to his defire, which I could not avoid
" faying was highly agreeable to myfelf

" The means by which we were to effect my
" enlargement I communicated to him, and were
" thefe; that when he returned an anfwer to my
" letter, he would put into the before-mentioned
" little bag, a cord, with which I could let down
" fome cloaths I fhould want, and fuppofed he
" could foon procure a ladder, which being fet
" to the window, I could eafily defcend, and
" fhould be happy to meet him at the bottom.

" Having made my letter weighty, and drop-
" ping it as before, I began to bufy myfelf with
" preparations I fpent that day and night [when
" I let down my bundle, compofed of fuch things as
" I fhould moft want] with much greater compofure
" than

"than I had known before for some time. My
"father paid me a visit. He came up in order
"to find if my sentiments continued the same.
"I answered to his interrogations with more re-
"solution than usual——from the latent hope
"this was the last trial I should have. but he
"soon turned my affected courage into real grief,
"when he told me, to-morrow morning I should
"be dragged to church, and he would force me
"to give my hand to Mr. Barker, if the next
"moment my final dissolution commenced.——
"What dreadful sounds were these to me, who
"had no hopes of escaping before the evening of
"that shocking morrow! I threw myself at his
"feet, telling him with streaming eyes, if he
"would grant me two or three days longer, I
"would then endeavour to oblige him. but that
"to-morrow, O my dearest father, my once
"kindest of parents, I cannot comply. For heaven's
"sake have compassion on my sufferings: and if
"I do not then chearfully acquiesce to your will,
"do with me as you think right.

"I fear, Madam, you will not acquit me of
"hypocrisy. but situated as I was, what could I
"do? there were no means, no subterfuges for
"me to escape the imminent danger which threat-
"ened me. and I was morally certain I should be
"out of their reach before that time.

"My father (a little softened by my intreaties
"and the agony he saw me in) swore then the day
"after should be the day of my nuptials.

"Glad was I when he left me, and turned the
"key of my door: tho' he protested he would
"keep me in ward 'till I was to be removed by
"a Habeas Corpus to Mr Barker's house.

"I added a few words, to advertise my lover
"of the danger I was near falling into. I did

Vol. I   D   "this,

" this, I own, from the motive of incitement,
" that he might be more expeditious. I had the
" felicity, as there was a little glimmering light
" from the moon, to find by a letter conveyed
" by the usual post, that every thing would be
" ready the next night by twelve precisely and
" at the distance of two fields, I should find a
" post-chaise, which would conduct me to a place
" of safety.

" I will pass over that night and the succeeding
" day, suffice it to say, that having put every
" thing I had of value or use that could go in a
" small compass in my pockets, I waited for the
" hour. Just as the clock struck twelve, I heard
" a little noise, I went softly to the window,
" which I gently lifted up, and finding a ladder
" placed there, I boldly ventured down, not
" without feeling some palpitation at taking a step
" that would undoubtedly be accounted rash and
" imprudent. But every doubt was hushed, and
" every fear dissipated, when I found myself at
" the bottom, and in the arms of the man I
" loved.

" He had with him a servant, who removed
" the ladder, and followed us. We found a chaise
" and four in waiting, into which we stept, and
" almost flew away. We travelled the remaining
" part of the night without stopping but I bore
" it with amazing spirits, tho' I had not taken
" any rest for some time,——owing to my con-
" tinual anxiety. " I begged of Captain Clayton
" not to spend much time in baiting, as I was
" apprehensive of a pursuit. Never woman had
" a more tender pleasing companion than myself.
" He would not suffer the least intruding thought
" that could give me pain, but was ever setting
" forth the happiness we should enjoy in one
                                        " another

" another and painted the blifs fond lovers tafte
" in the moft glowing colors

" I have fince recollected he did not talk of
" matrimony, however, that did not occur to
" me at the time, nor fhould I have taken notice
" of it, if it had not doubting but we were on
" our way to Scotland, and our marriage when
" we arrived thither as an event of courfe

" To avoid confufion, I muft tell you, it was
" on Monday my father firft confined me, and
" on Friday that I made my efcape On Satur-
" day night I lay down in my cloaths, and flept
" about two hours I may fafely fay, that was
" the only good reft I had been fenfible of from
" the time of my father's quarrelling with Captain
" Clayton

" We ftill profecuted our journey with the
" fame rapidity I cannot help here remarking,
" Captain Clayton feemed to me to be much
" more free in his behaviour than I had ever
" known him, and talked in a manner which fa-
" voured of libertinifm. I thought it would be
" the beft method to appear not to underftand
" him, but I could not long maintain my pretence
" of ignorance, I then told him, I was appre-
" henfive I had harboured miftaken notions of
" him,———or rather my too ready compliance
" with his folicitations, had given him a mean
" opinion of my virtue but I was willing, both
" for his fake and my own, to hope he only
" meant this alarming behaviour as a trial of that
" virtue he might affure himfelf was impregnable.

" He took my hand, and preffing it to his
" bofom, fwore he believed he had an angel with
" him, and endeavoured to excufe his behaviour,
" faying, My deareft Lucy, had I been deceived
" in your amiable goodnefs, I had been the moft

" wretched

"wretched of all human beings what felicity
"may I not hope to taste with a wife of such
"sentiments! I soon——too soon suffered my
"rising fears to be hushed, and believed the
"man my soul doated on to be all I fondly
"wished him.
"I am now, Madam, coming to a part of my
"history, which may truly be called melancholy;
"and am convinced, that it is not in the power
"of grief alone to kill; for could that put a pe-
"riod to our lives, mine would have been ere
"now at an end. I should not now have been
"lamenting my misfortunes.
"This fatal night, the last of all my earthly
"hopes of happiness, we arrived at an inn about
"nine o'clock. Captain Clayton left me, to or-
"der somewhat for supper, and returned to me
"with a bowl of punch in his hand——would
"it had been poison, for that could only have
"killed my mortal part, but this fatal draught,
"which by his persuasion, and my being excesĺ-
"sively thirsty, I drank largely of, was meant
"to blast all my hopes of happiness both here
"and hereafter!——I thought at the time it was
"not pleasant, but my great drought prevented
"my taking much notice of it——I very soon
"felt myself extremely sleepy, I complained of
"it. Captain Clayton said, he was so too, from
"the fatigues we had undergone.
"I soon wished my companion a good night
"and attended by a woman servant, went to my
"chamber. I found such an uncommon drowsi-
"ness come over me, I had scarce power to un-
"dress myself it did not however alarm me,
"since I thought I could so readily account for
"it. I fell into a sound sleep as soon as in bed——
"Oh that I had never awoke!——O Madam!
"how

"how shall I tell you? How can I exprefs my
"horror and anguifh when I waked, and found
"myfelf in the arms of the wretch who had
"fworn to guard and protect me! The defpair I
"felt, cannot by you be conceived I fhrieked,
"ftruggled,—— intreated and raved by turns;
"one moment begging the monfter to leave me,
"the next, loading him with juft reproaches of
"his bafenefs He ufed all the arts he was maf-
"ter of to calm me, and fwore that he would
"marry me I bid him leave me, and let me
"never more behold a cruel wretch, who had fo
"bafely forfeited all pretenfions to honor and
"faith He then, thinking to appeafe me, plead-
"ed the violence of his paffion, and the irrefifti-
"blenefs of my charms· but all he could urge
"was of no effect. I continued my cries, which,
"however, ferved no other purpofe than to wafte
"my ftrength, for I had but too much reafon to
"fear no one in that vile houfe would give me
"affiftance; as it was proved to me from Clay-
"ton's gaining admittance into my room, I hav-
"ing the preceding evening locked the door.

"By my exceffive ftruggling to free myfelf
"from the detefted wretch, joined to my afflicti-
"on of mind, my ftrength and fpirits were in-
"tirely exhaufted, and I fell into a ftrong fit;—
"the man who had robbed me of all I held dear,
"and reduced me to that dreadful fituation, could
"not behold me in the agonies of death, as he
"thought,—which, were he poffeffed of the leaft
"feelings of humanity, he fhould rather have
"wifhed,—without ufing every method to reftore
"me to that life I wifhed to lofe: fearing I fhould
"relapfe at the fight of a man I had fo much
"reafon to hate, he left the room as foon as the
"woman fervant made her appearance. Her pre-

"fence

" fence was odious to me, I bad her be gone to
" the vile monster who had fent her, and pufhed
" her out of the room So fearful was I that
" Clayton would make me another vifit, that I
" dragged a cheft of drawers in my fright, and
" placed it againft the door, which fome time
" after I could hardly remove by my utmoft et
" forts

" I dreffed myfelf haftily, hardly knowing what
" I was about I wonder indeed I kept my fenfes,
" but my grief took fuch various turns, as muft
" be the reafon of my preferving them At one
" time I would ftamp about the room, and call
" aloud for my undoer, proclaiming my cruel
" wrongs; then throw myfelf upon the floor,
" tearing my cloaths and hair One time I ftart-
" ed up, and running to the window, fhould
" have precipitated myfelf headlong down—but
" heaven, ever merciful, prevented my adding
" felf-murder to my other crimes ——Shocked at
" my attempt, I burft into a flood of tears, and
" proftrating myfelf on the ground, I implored
" forgivenefs of God, but almoft inftantaneoufly
" arofe, becaufe I could not help mixing curfes
" on the head of the bafe Clayton, with my pe-
" titions for myfelf I fat now quite ftupified
" with the violence of my affliction, when I was
" roufed by the wretch pleading at the door to
" be heard one moment · all that man could fay,
" he did, fwearing he would leave me 'till, by
" the moft fevere penance I could impofe on him,
" he had expiated his crime I bid him leave
" perfecuting me, his idea was odious I would
" die rather than behold the wretch who had fo
" irreparably injured me He then endeavoured
" to prove by the moft elaborate rhetoric, that
" my mind being ftill pure, I had fuftained no

" injury

"injury at all that what had happened to me,
"had to thoufands before, who were neverthelefs
"very happy in marriage Did not all young
"women, who go with men to Scotland, run the
"fame rifk? and would not all men avail them-
"felves of the latitude given them?——I bad
"him be filent, his words were daggers to my
"heart He had robbed me of my innocence
"and peace of mind I had nothing now dear
"to me to lofe Why did he folicit my hand?
"Could I have refolved to have given that with-
"out my heart, I fhould not be now lamenting
"my lofs of honor That my former efteem
"and affection were changed into deadly hate and
"deteftation, fentiments which I wou'd cherifh
"the remainder of my wretched life which a
"too fatal dependence on his faith had made fo.
"Could I, after fo flagrant a proof of his bafe
"depravity, confent to marry him, I fhould then
"become vile as himfelf, that I would embrace
"death in the moft dreadful form, ere I would,
"if poffible, fet my eyes on him that this was
"my final refolution and rather than fubject
"myfelf to his hated prefence, I would put an
"end to that life, which was become of no ac-
"count with me,——fince I had loft all that made
"it valuable

"Whether he was apprehenfive I fhould put
"my threats in execution,——or from what mo-
"tive I know not, but he left the door.

"I was much intreated to partake of fome re-
"frefhment, but refufed and tho' I took no man-
"ner of fuftenance that day, I had no craving of
"nature Exclufive of the agony of my mind,
"I had a very difagreeable tafte and drynefs in
"my mouth, occafioned, as I have fince thought,

"by the sleepy potion which had been administer-
"ed to me the night before

"In the afternoon he rode out, and returned
"not 'till late: however, he tormented me not
"with his base persuasions. Ah, how odious
"does vice make people! The man, whom the
"day before I beheld with adoration, appeared
"now the most shocking object imaginable: and
"nothing possessed my thoughts, but to find
"some method of flying from him.

"I had great reason to believe, the woman
"who had been accessary to my ruin, was one of
"those mercenary wretches, who would under-
"take any thing for the lucre of gain. I did not
"therefore doubt but she would further my escape,
"in order to gain a larger sum of Captain Clayton
"for my recovery. I found the next morning, he
"was to go out for the whole day, I therefore
"spoke to the maid, telling her I would give her
"a sum of money, if she would suffer me to get
"away: adding, I was convinced Captain Clay-
"ton loved me sincerely, and that I as sincerely
"forgave him: and owned, I did not see this af-
"fair in so bad a light now, as I did at first, but
"that my pride would not suffer me to make any
"advances towards a reconciliation—tho' it was
"what I ardently longed for. but if I could se-
"crete myself any where for a few hours, he
"would, by his impatience to regain me, give
"her a larger bribe, and she might acquaint him
"where I was, so that he would then have an
"opportunity of seemingly forcing me to do what
"in reality I had as great an inclination to do as
"himself

"Stupid, and unlikely to gain credit as this
"story was, it yet had some weight with this
"abandoned woman, who could never believe
"any

' any one would make such a rout as she said
' about nothing at all. and promised me the first
' opportunity of a clear stage to let me out. I
' gave her two guineas, by way of earnest, with
' the promise of four more when I left the house.
' I asked her what place I might go to a little way
' from thence. she named some place not far off,
' because, said she, Captain Clayton will be in a
' monstrous passion when he misses you

" I took some breakfast, and secured two rolls
" in my pockets according to promise, she let me
" out, and described the place of rendezvous suf-
" ficiently clear to me to avoid it, which I did
" with great caution

" The first person I met, I enquired how far it
" was to the next town he answered, eight
" miles, but there was a returned chaise going
" thither I thanked him for his information
" with an assumed calmness, for fear of creating
" suspicion, and said, if the boy and I could agree
" for a trifle, I would take that method. The
" post-chaise instantly came in sight, I hastily
" stepped into it, and bid the boy drive with all
" expedition, and I would reward him. When I
" came to the town, I took another, and went
" twenty miles across the country, where I rested
" that night, thinking myself more secure than if
" I had gone on to London.

" From hence I wrote to a lady in the town
" where I had lived, intreating her to inform me
" how my absconding was received by my family:
" and whether I might hope to be forgiven by
" them? likewise to beg her to direct to me under
" a feigned name, to be left at the post-house in
" S——— In about ten days, I received an an-
" swer

" fwer, wherein I was told, it was reprefented
" I had abufed the tendernefs of the beft of pa
" rents,——had had an intrigue with Captai,
" Clayton, and being fearful of the confequences,
" had eloped with him —That I muft never pre
' fume to come into that part of the country
" again, as my father would profecute Captain
" Clayton and myfelf for a robbery, in having
" broke open a bureau,—which however wa,
" falfe ———Thus was every refource cut off
" My money began to run fhort ; however, I
" parted with a few valuables, and took a place
" in the London ftage not that I knew what to
" do when I came there, but I was reduced by
" this intelligence to defpair Juft before I ar-
" rived at this village, I was feized with a violent
" giddinefs in my head, and fickifhnefs I wis
" forced to quit the coach, and fome people led
" me to this farm-houfe my illnefs encreafed fo
" much, that I could not think of profecuting the
" journey, I therefore accepted this good woman's
" kind invitation of lodging with her 'till I was
" better I have been here above a month and
' could I forget what has befallen me, with the
" profpect before me, I might hope to be eafy
" ———happinefs, I am convinced, can never be
" my lot
" I have certainly, Madam, tired you with my
" melancholy detail if you can acquit me of
" actual guilt, it is all the favor I think you can
" allow me but the deepeft contrition I fhall
" ever feel I hope heaven will pardon the fuf-
" fering myfelf to be deceived, where I had placed
" a too unlimited confidence "

I comforted the fair· penitent all in my power,
both from compaffion for her fufferings, and an inclination which I feel for her

October

October 22

I have just read your letter, your account of your picture is very picturesque. I forgive the detention, considering in whose hands it was, had I been the man, I should not so easily have parted with it.

Indeed, my lovely Caroline, you must not give way to your ahs! and ohs! I will not allow it. I cannot believe it is in the power of any man to converse freely with such a woman as my Caroline, and remain insensible of her many charms ---your picture being so long detained by Darnley, confirms my former opinion that he loves you, and only waits a proper time to make the interesting discovery.

But you shall not be melancholy ---A fine cure for the vapors tho', to be sure, this poor girl's story ---Why should this same passion " sweet passion of love" make such horrid *mopuses* of us poor women? Why, because we feel a partiality for a pretty fellow of the lordly sex, must every breath usher in a sigh, and a moment's solitude a tear?
" 'Tis strange, 'tis passing strange."

Now for your Sidney, who knows not what love means ---That has been granted you may remember,---she only cherishes a reverence, let me call it, for the memory of an amiable man---he is dead you know to all intents and purposes to me,-- But the cherishing this reverence---or what you will, has preserved my heart whole in the midst of dangers. Not the lovely Darnley, not the amiable Evelin can---nor do they, I dare say, wish they could---make any impression on my heart. Upon my honor, in general the whole sex is hardly worth our care. I don't think I could mention six who merit favor from any of us.

Adieu,

Adieu, my love: accept my thanks for the dear picture.

Your's

SIDNEY VERE.

LETTER XX.

TO MISS VERE.

Grosvenor-Square, October 27.

I Have this instant perused your pacquet.---An adventure indeed! poor unhappy creature! To what dreadful misfortunes does one false step lead us! What a disappointment to her fair prospects! By your timely assistance you may have preserved her from greater ills.---I am sorry you have not your father's concurrence. Men have not that delicacy of sentiment in those affairs as we have. I hope, however, Sir William will not oppose your kind intention of succouring the distressed fugitive.--Ah! how cruel were the parents of Miss Arnold, inhumanely to urge their child to such proceedings!---But what words can express the indignation which fills my heart, when the reflection of the infamous Clayton's baseness recurs to me! horrid, premeditated villain! And yet perhaps, my Sidney, this wretch, who dares to trample on every law human and divine, is received with pleasure in all societies. Detestable monster! what punishment can equal his desert. Were such men shunned, and treated by every one as they merit, it would certainly in some measure be a means of putting an end to their vile practices.

In the society of Miss Arnold, I doubt not you will find an agreeable companion.—Sensible she seems to be from her narrative. She is fortunate in meeting such a friend in her affliction as you.—My Sidney knows to distinguish between an actual fault, and an unintentional one.

I am afraid there are some ladies of our acquaintance, who would be so outrageously virtuous as to shudder at the bare apprehension of being seen with Miss Arnold, and yet, to their shame, would say of the wretch who has reduced her to this misery, " 'tis pity he is so gay, for he is a fine fellow." It is the only proof some women give of their own virtue, degrading and vilifying those who have lost it, not reflecting on the circumstances attending their fall. I should be afraid to declare my sentiments on this head, to any but yourself.—I feel in myself a greater propensity to pity those unfortunate women who swerve from virtue's rule, than many of my sex will allow their due. But what besides arbitrary custom can obsolve a man from a crime which renders a woman infamous? or why is it deemed dishonourable for one to grant what it is the glory of the other to solicit? Not that I exculpate either from guilt but then let the greatest shame fall on them who are undoubtedly most guilty.

Miss Arnold's case is however widely different; her mind is free from blemish still virtuous,—— but still can never know happiness. the cruel villain has destroyed all hopes of that. What an aggravation to her misfortunes must be the reflection that they were occasioned by a man on whom her soul reposed! perhaps too, she still harbours too much tenderness for him she cannot at once divest herself of the soft sentiments she used to indulge for one so base. Her unhappy situation is

truly

truly deplorable! I need not remind my Sidney of softening, in the moſt delicate manner, her griefs I know your ſweetly-ſoothing-ſympathetic ſoul, or you could not bear with your Caroline's weakneſs Ah, my Sidney! ſhe is ſtill the ſame weak creature—ſtill loves—ſtill doubts—yet ſtill indulges frail hope My ſweet flatterer, why do you urge me on to further deceit?

How have I wandered—why did you not check me—in the flowery path, 'till I found myſelf drawn imperceptibly to too great a length; and then turning, find an immeaſurable way behind, not to be repaſſed—and before me, nothing but thorns and briars, which intercept my road to happineſs

Since the adventure of the picture, I have caught Sir George looking earneſtly at me he has dropped his eyes when he found himſelf diſcovered Ah, why does he ſuffer his eyes to dwell upon me! Can he, my Sidney, be waiting for an opportunity?—Ah!—but you ſay you will not have any more ahs! and ohs!—it is a great relief in expreſſion, ſuperior to heigh-ho!—I will endeavour to obey you but, that I may be certain of not offending, will conclude here Believe me

ever your's,

CAROLINE MELMOTH

LETTER

LETTER XXI.

To Miss Vire.

Grovesner-Square, November 6.

I Spent this day in St James's-Square. The first part of it, I thought myself happy; the latter part convinced me I was otherwise. From some circumstances, I was tempted to give way to the fond belief you contributed to raise in my bosom, that Sir George really only wanted an opportunity to disclose—what?—Ah, my Sidney! how ready are we to delude ourselves!

And yet his words,——his looks, more than his words, have for some time been particular: he pays me such compliments,---tho' without appearing to design them as such.---But what avail his kind expressions or tender looks,——in vain for me, they are kind and tender! difficulties, unsurmountable, oppose themselves to my presumptuous hopes, and to his——perhaps too great sensibility.

Miss Darnley had engaged me to go with her and her sister to Langford's auction to-day at one o'clock. I was with Mrs Grafton, reading to her and Miss Grafton. About twelve, Sir George Darnley called on us. he told me " his sisters were prevented going to the auction; but that they might not be sensible of their disappointment, beg of you to spend the day with them: they have" added he, " deputed me to convey you to St James's-Square, knowing, I was to pay a visit in your neighbourhood, and should be happy in being your escorte."

I told Sir George, I was much obliged to him, and looked at Mrs Grafton, as if for permission. She

She underſtood me By all means, my dear Caroline is ready to attend you, Sir George, wherever you pleaſe "

We chatted very agreeably about half an hour, and then we ſet off He led me down ſtairs How ſilly I was!—The knowledge of my being to be alone with him,—and your " want of opportunity" ruſhed into my mind together I trembled and tottered down the ſteps.—Frederick had not got the footſtep of the chariot quite down,—I, not ſenſible of it, was hurrying in —Sir George preſſ-ed the hand he ſtill held, with gentle vehemence Stop, my Caroline, one inſtant!—The words,—the accent,—the preſſure, added to my perturba-tion—I felt the color mount up in my face the conſcioufneſs of bluſhing increaſes it —My confuſi-on was augmented by my aukwardneſs in getting into the chariot I miſſed the ſtep, and was near falling, however, I recovered myſelf by the help of Sir George.

When we were ſeated, he tenderly inquired it I had hurt myſelf, I returned an anſwer in the negative · " I am glad of it !" ſaid he earneſtly,—and looking in my face, " I would not have you ſuffer the leaſt pain for the univerſe " I aſſured him, I was not ſenſible of any and added, if I was, I muſt impute it to my aukwardneſs We were then both ſilent

Have you, my dear Sidney, ever experienced the ſituation I found myſelf in, of thinking it ne-ceſſary you ſhould ſay ſome indifferent thing or other, in order to make a ſubject, and look firſt out of one window,—and then the other glaſs, to receive, if poſſible, ſome helps from what paſſes before you, fix on a thouſand, and reject them as faſt, yet ſtill continue ſilent: and tho' every mo-ment it becomes more irkſome, and more necef-

ſary,

fary, the difficulties increase with the lengthening silence? Thus did we drive up one street, and down another. At last Sir George broke the charm by asking how your ladyship did this was a happy question, a subject on which I could expatiate freely I did. I enumerated all your perfections, and expressed the happiness your friendship conferred on me " Miss Vere is a sweet, amiable girl," said he, " and is a very great favorite of mine, I assure you" " That man," said I, " who can call my Sidney his, will be the happiest of men!'" " One of the happiest," returned Sir George· " I admire Miss Vere, but there are women besides, whose amiable qualities, from their diffident modesty unknown to himselves, or only allowed in others, whose choice may he deemed happy in the superlative degree what say you Miss Melmoth," taking my hand, " don't you know one such woman, Miss Vere excepted?" " Many, Sir"---not attempting to withdraw my hand, lest it should look like a consciousness of I know-not-what —Ah, Sidney! surely here was no want of opportunity? " Many, sir, there are," I answered " but at the time I spoke, my ideas of perfection were all centered in my dear Sidney." Your dear Sidney," repeated Sir George, " so you really love your Sidney, better than any one in the world beside?" This was a hard question to answer sincerely.—My hand still continued in his,—passively, I may say. under pretence of adjusting a pin in my cloak, I removed it He made no attempt to detain it.—But the question was still unanswered " Why yes, Sir George, Miss Vere possesses the highest share of my friendship" " I am glad to find," replied he, " you make a distinction between friendship and love" " There are degrees of both, I believe". [I simply rejoined. And yet, false and foolish as

my

my anfwer was—for in true love can there be degrees?—it feemed a tacit acknowledgment, that I was a ftranger to that paffion, (and fo ferved my purpofe,) a belief I would wifh to inculcate in every one, for, amiable as Sir George Darnley is, I could not bear the reflection, that even he fhould difcover my partiality, which, if I cannot fubdue, I muft at leaft endeavour to conceal] " Are there" afked he in return " I fhould think not We may indeed ftrive to make fuch, but a fincere paffion can know no bounds it may indeed be concealed, for filent love, like filent water, is deepeft "—Heaven knows when he would have ended,—or how much farther he would have gone, for he had juft refumed my hand, and feemed going on, when the coachman turned fhort out of York-ftreet, to avoid another carriage, by which he had very near thrown the chariot over, and as the fhock was on my fide, almoft threw me into the arms of his mafter—So the " opportunity," Sidney, was loft for two minutes brought us to Lady Darnley's

After dinner, we were all chatting very pleafantly on various fubjects, when the difcourfe imperceptibly turned on love Sir George, I thought fpoke feelingly I liftened with mute attention, like the drowning wretch who catches at ever ftraw He difplayed great eloquence " I hate people arguing without being mafters of their fubject," faid Harriot " You talk of love, brother, I dare fay, you were never ferioufly in love in your life " " Why muft I be in love ferioufly, Harriot? Love is all hope, and hope is joy one may love fervently, without being fo very ferious, —or looking fo, as Mifs Melmoth does at this inftant "—" Who I? I was all attention to the converfation,' faid I, blufhing, and looking more filly than ferious, I believe if poffible.

" Well,"

„ Well," said Louisa, " I still believe Sir George has left his heart abroad, or else nature has formed him without one,—as she is said to do some folks without brains "

Never," said Sir George, " was there a truer observation than that women cannot get together without discoursing of love "

" Pray who began the conversation ?—Was it not you, Sir George ? Then why do you blame us poor women, when yourself, one of the Lords of the Creation, was the cause of the subject coming on the tapis "—" That I might be the first," he replied, " who spoke upon the subject, I will not attempt to deny but who was the occasion of it ?— even yourself, you looked so charmingly lovely, that to gaze on you and think of love, was the same thing. and out of the abundance of the heart,—I remember something good, you see "—" Your memory serves to very little purpose then, Sir George, since you endeavour to pervert the intention of the bible, which was not meant to raise vanity "

" Upon my word, Sir George," said Lady Darnley, " if Miss Caroline had not more sense than most of her sex, you would make her vain but she knows you are a giddy young fellow, and never speak to pretty women as you mean "

I bowed to her ladyship and said, " she would go nearer to make me have too good an opinion of myself, since she flattered my vanity more than any one could by praising my person "

" But," said Harriot, " we have run from our subject You, Louisa, was saying, you fancied my brother had left his heart with some lady abroad "—True, I did, nor do I dissent from my assertion for if he had not, what could protect him from feeling the influence of so many beauties

as

as we have to vifit us? There is lady Amelia Stanton. a lovely perfon,—fine accomplifhments, and a great fortune. Mifs Grafton too "—" So, you imagine, my dear fifter, that the man who can behold thefe two ladies with indifference, muft, if he has travelled, have parted with his heart? Is it a neceffary confequence,—becaufe a lady, whom you have fingled out, does not fuit my tafte, that there is no other in England could make me happy."

"Not at all, brother but I muft own, it is rather fingular, that out of all your acquaintance— joined to the earneft defire my mother and we have to fee you married—you fhould not have been tempted to make an election."

"Perhaps," faid he, fmiling, "there may be fo many candidates, I fhould not know on whom to fix my choice For inftance, there is your friend lady Amelia,—and feveral others I could name,— all equally charming,—and alike equally indifferent."

"I wifh I could find out what fort of a woman my brother likes," faid Harriot——" Will like" interrupted Louifa, for it does not appear that he likes any one yet "——" And 'till it does appear," faid Sir George, " let us never more talk ferioufly on this fubject"

" As this is then to be the laft time," faid Lady Darnley, " I will difmifs it, after begging leave to fay a few words It would give me the higheft fatisfaction this world can afford, to fee all my children happily and properly married by the laft expreffion I mean, fo as not to have any caufe to reflect upon themfelves, for flighting the moft material points, when too late.

" There muft, in all alliances, be a profpect of felicity. Riches, we all know, alone eannot confti

tute

tute happiness, but as our families of either side have never degenerated, I hope I shall not live to have the inexpressible mortification of seeing the pure stream, which has run through so many generations, stained by my childrens marrying contrary to their birth and real expectations. You are all brothers and sisters here, remember."— With these words she ended, looking round upon us. I know not whether it were really so, but I thought her eyes dwelt longest on me. I could not help making the application to myself. Good God! how could I dare to think of staining their pure stream with my plebeian blood! What a lesson for me! Sidney, I am not to possess the common blessings of mankind. Ignorant of my birth, I must likewise be incapable of sensibility. A mere worm! My faculties seemed all suspended. I was lost in cogitation, when I was awakened by Sir George Darnley saying, " he wished the conversation had not been carried so far, as it had made us all grave;" and added, it was the best way not to come to explanations, when we are not certain our thoughts may coincide. Then taking out his watch, said he had an engagement, which he had near forgotten,—begged our excuse, and bowing with great form to all,—to me in particular——took his hat and sword, and went out ——

——And there, my Sidney, went all my hopes Hopes! how could I be so absurd as to permit them ever to gain footing in my breast? Ah, ye cruel invaders of my peace! why cannot I root ye out? But they are too firmly fixed there, to be removed by the gentle efforts I make; and my heart is become so tender, it would break were I to use harsh methods.

I thought once or twice, while his mother was speaking, Sir George looked with tender attention on me—but we are brother and fifters, what a qualifying way fome people have!—and a brother may behold his fifter with looks of brotherly love—I wifhed to poffefs his efteem, I have a fhare in it. Why cannot I be contented? I wifh him all happinefs. I have afked my heart, if I could fupport the feeing him married,—fuppofe to Mifs Grafton, my blood turns chill, and I am ready to fink; then I fay, fuppofe I fhould ever difcover my parents, and they fhould be found in nothing inferior to the Darnley family; a fever takes poffeffion of my whole frame,——my face glows, —my heart beats e'en to burfting, 'till awaking from my trance of fancied happinefs, I find. I feel myfelf wretched; but left I fhould make you fo, will conclude

Your's faithfully,

CAROLINE MELMOTH.

LETTER XXII.

To Mifs VERE.

Grofvenor-Square, November 23.

I AM quite alone; forfaken by all my friends, except my ever kind benefactrefs; all the Darnley family are gone to Bath. Mifs Grafton is of their party.

How is it, my dear, that I could remain free from any difquietude, when you were in company with Sir George Darnley, and yet feel an anxiety, left Mifs Grafton fhould captivate his heart? It appears ftrangely fingular to me; for you have the fuperiority over her infinitely, both in perfon and accomplifhments!—that you muft own yourfelf, becaufe you will not allow Letitia to be at all
handfome

handsome. How can I account for this---what-shall-I call-it?---perhaps thus, you would not endeavour to make an interest in his bosom detrimental to your Caroline, nor would you strive to please—but do we please, by striving to please?—Alas! I fear the contrary.——Miss Grafton, I am afraid, loves him,—or at least would not be displeased with his loving her.—You have no views,—she has many.——What opportunities has she now! I so few—and those lost! Happy girl!

"The lucky have whole days, which still they chuse,
"Th' unlucky have but hours, and those they lose."

But after all, should he really possess all the tenderness in the world for me, 'tis plain his family would be against me. They think not of any such thing. They cannot form an idea, that the heir of their ancient house could look on such an one as me. Ought I then to wish he should love me? Yet I should speak falsely, were I to say, I wish he did not. I would die to save him from pain. But ah! there must be such exquisite pleasure in being reciprocally beloved, as would recompense an age of doubt. I could be happy in the the thought, that were it possible to surmount the obstacles placed in our way,—that he would live for me alone, contented would I live alone for him.—This is not a Platonic passion, Sidney; but it is pure and rational.——I might perhaps be able to say some things more in favour of my rationality, but you will lose the advantage of reading, and edifying, no doubt—by being summoned to dinner. Adieu à present.

Eleven o'Clock.

Lady Alicia Montague, who you know is a particular friend of Mrs Grafton's, has long wanted that lady to accompany her to Montague-lodge, in Hertfordshire. She has at length consented—Mrs Grafton does not like taking me down with them. She thinks " the company of two old women," she says, " cannot be pleasing to a young one, tho' she should never discover it, owing to her good sense and politeness." I answered, " I should have very little of those qualities, if I did not think they conferred honor on me, in taking me with them."

" My dear Caroline, I expected no less from you; but you may be much happier with your friend at Vere-Park. I must not always ingross you to myself. If I do not now and then use myself to a little absences from you, how shall I support a final one. Dear as you are to me, I shall scarcely miss you while in the society of my dear Lady Alicia; or if I should, the reflection that you are both reaping advantage and pleasure, will compensate the separation ——Your Sidney will thank me for resigning you to her. It would be cruel, while all the christian world is in joy, to immure you in the society only of dulness and old age."

Will you, Sidney, accept of my company? I shall not however wait for your answer; I can do that for you myself. Your father will not retract his obliging invitation; besides you have told me, I am a great favorite of his.

There is something very affecting in Lady Alicia's history; so I believe we shall find on enquiry in every body's——She has been a very fine figure, and is so still, I may say, considering her age, being turned of seventy; but possesses all her faculties better than many do in the meridian of life.

She

She does me the honor of conversing frequently with me. I always leave her with regret, but greatly edified.

Lady Alicia gave me yesterday a little sketch of her story — I will repeat it to you in her words.

"When about sixteen, I was addressed by a young nobleman — Sixteen is an age, my dear, when girls are apt to fall in love — I may truly say, I was so with Lord B — My father wished us to wait 'till I was eighteen, before I undertook the cares of a family,—women at that time were more domestic than they are now. Lord B had frequent access to our house; my friends looked on him as already one of the family.

"I had not then the happiness of knowing our dear Mrs Grafton; but I had a bosom-friend. First friends, like first loves, are seldom permanent, because seldom chosen with judgment. Of this friend, however, I was extravagantly fond. I never concealed a thought from her.—She proved unfaithful. I had broken vows, and a false friend's treachery, to mourn at the same time. I lost my lover and friend together. I was severely afflicted at my double disappointment. My lord had not declared himself above six months; a year and a half was a long time to stay,—my friend was not so scrupulous. They were married before I gave myself leave to suspect an alteration in the sentiments of them.

"I used all my philosophy and religion—which answered my purpose best—to conquer a love and friendship so ill placed and requited. The task was hard, but the triumph was greater, when achieved, from the difficulty. I at length succeeded. My heart became perfectly serene, and perhaps that serenity was augmented by the reflection that I had

had tasted the reverse. I lived quietly in my father's house, with not a wish beyond his walls.

"About a year, or a little more, from this time, I was invited to the wedding of a young lady, a distant relation to me, who was to be married to Lord L grandfather to the present—I there first saw Miss Melmoth, who, though three years younger than myself, instantly took my notice. I there likewise saw, for the first time, Mr Montague, brother to the Earl of L.

"Friendship and love had ever an equal interest in my bosom. An intimacy with Miss Melmoth, which can end but with our lives, commenced from that day, and an attachment to Mr Montague soon took place. His merit sufficiently justified my partiality for him, as Mrs Grafton's has done my friendship for her.

"I continued some time at Lord L's. Mr Montague was the most amiable of men. I should have been insensible as well as ungrateful, had not his tender assiduities made an impression on me: they did; I yielded to his persuasions; and my reason confirmed and approved my choice.

"He was the most tender, the most faithful of men. His passion for me could only be equalled by my affection for him. How different was his behaviour from Lord B's! How different my attachment to him!

"What happy days we passed together!---My friends had but one objection, and that was a proof of their tenderness; Mr Montague bore a colonel's commission---my father had been a soldier in his youth, and my mother could not bear her daughter should experience the grief she had endured from the absence of her lord.—Mr. Montague was very willing to resign his commission—Europe was then at peace—his glory, his happiness centered

tered in being a good man in private life. He was prepared to give up the command of his regiment when the rebellion broke out. George the First was scarcely seated on his throne. The families on both sides were firmly attached to the Hanoverian line, but to have thrown up his commission at such a juncture, would have been giving very little proof of his loyalty. Mr Montague had however a severe conflict between love and duty. My silent, tho' painful acquiescence to the calls of his duty, as it raised his admiration, encreased his difficulties.

"My God! what were my feelings at our approaching separation! His regiment was ordered to march on that day which had been fixed for our union. Mr Montague begged to have the ceremony performed, but my father and mother opposed it. I ever paid the most implicit obedience to them—for the first time, I found difficulty in complying with their will.

"The evening before his departure, Mr. Montague visited me in my dressing room. we were scarcely able to speak. He threw himself on his knees, and, in the most pathetic manner, intreated me to receive his hand. the reflection that I was irrevocably his, he said, would sweeten every hardship—A beloved lover, pleading with all the eloquence of passion at our feet, with our hearts on his side, is irresistible—My Montague was so to me. I consented the chaplain should join our hands, on condition he would leave me immediately after the ceremony had passed. He only wished to secure me to himself, and would have have subscribed to impossibilities—We were married, and he tore himself from me.

"The next morning was the last I was to behold him. Great God! how dreadful was our parting! —still

—still does the remembrance wring my heart — still do I see his clasped hands,—pale looks,—and starting tears still hear his prayers in a voice scarcely articulate to the throne of grace for our speedy meeting —Ah! they reached not the throne of grace —we met no more My dear, my faithful Montague, my husband fell, fighting for his king, covered with wounds in the last decisive battle He gained immortal glory but oh! was the never-fading laurel a balsam for a broken heart? Could his brave actions dry my tears, when by his bravery he lost his life, and I the best of men! Ah! what availed it to me, he did thus, or thus, those who repeated his exploits, had a tale to tell, which obliterated all—My Montague, the friend of mankind, was slain!

" Life was a burden to me many years I saw nobody, except my dear Marianne She was my only comforter, because she soothed my grief,— indulged me in talking of my Montague, and mingled her tears with mine she too wept for her cousin, whom she dearly loved

" My father and mother forgave, or rather forgot to chide me, for marrying Mr Montague I retired to his house, which he left me, together with his estate in Hertfordshire, by a will he made immediately after our union Several matches were proposed to me, but I rejected them all — I had one answer At length I was left being persecuted I was determined to remain a virgin-widow for my Montague's sake."

This little narrative affected me exceedingly — I wept ——Lady Alicia's tears coursed each other down her cheeks ——Every circumstance appears before her eyes, altho' 'tis fifty years since Mr. Montague's death ——Mrs Grafton and Lady Alicia propose setting out for Montague-lodge on
the

the 5th of December. On that day, unless you forbid me, I shall leave London, and haste to my Sidney. Adieu.

CAROLINE MELMOTH.

LETTER XXIII.

To Miss VERE.

Grosvenor-square, February 23.

THE pleasure I received on seeing my friends in town, has met with a little allay. You remember the late Mr Melmoth's housekeeper resided since his death with Mrs Grafton, in the same capacity. When I arrived here, I enquired for Mrs Johnson, but was told by Henry, "she had been discharged above a month." "Discharged!" I exclaimed, "for what?" "He said, he could never rightly understand; but that his lady thought herself very ill used by Mrs Johnson—and was determined to hear nothing in her favor."

Notwithstanding this determination, I was determined to have a trial whether Mrs Grafton would hear any thing in her favor. I did not much reckon upon what Henry said, as I knew none of the servants would risk their lady's anger, by vindicating her: she had been too faithful to Mrs Grafton's interest, not to have enemies among them. I therefore mentioned my concern to Mrs Grafton.—She said, "she had found Mrs Johnson to be a very artful creature, who had made much mischief in the family; and had likewise wronged her.—That she had sent her off; and was resolved to part with any servant, who should hold any correspondence with her. indeed" she added, "they know my determination so well, that not one of them have offered a word in her behalf."

"It seems altogether very amazing to me, Madam, that Mrs Johnson could have altered so much in such a short time,—have turned out such an ungraceful woman."—"I have long seen it," interrupted Miss Grafton.—I continued "Surely, she must have been misrepresented to you—she has enemies, who have abused your ear." "My dear," returned Mrs Grafton, "you will oblige me, by saying no more about her —she is very undeserving of any one's care. I am sorry she remained so long here."—"Pardon me, Madam, but indeed I cannot have so bad an opinion of poor Mrs Johnson." "You do not well, Caroline, to oppose your opinion to my judgment." "Indeed, my dearest Madam, I meant not to do so; it would be very arrogant in me, to pretend to do it; and still farther from my intention. And yet—you must, my kind benefactress, forgive your child,—when I reflect on the dutiful behaviour and respect Mrs Johnson ever paid you." —"Surely, Miss Melmoth, you stand not in need of being twice reminded.—Your earnest vindication of an unworthy creature, however great your obligations to her,—gives but little proof of your gratitude to my aunt."

"Every one, Miss Grafton, knows my obligation to Mrs Johnson; she it was who introduced an unhappy little infant to the best of families. I do not forget my origin, Miss Grafton. I needed not therefore to be twice reminded." I was vexed, my countenance shewed it, as well as my words.

"Your warmth, my dear Caroline, does not please me. By vindicating wicked people, we become partakers with them in their faults. I am satisfied with my own proceedings. Do you learn
to

to be so too,-- or at least appear so to me ---I took my niece's advice. Had you been in town, I should likewise have asked yours." "I wish I had, madam, you would have done me great honor, and perhaps"---" I will not hear another word. Let us change the discourse." Which she did, by asking me how I employed my time while at Vic-Park.

This morning I rose early, and went to Mrs Johnson's lodgings. The poor woman wept when she saw me. "Ah! my dear Miss Melmoth, I should not have been discharged, at least not so disgracefully, if you had been at home. Thank God, but half their malice succeeded. I am contented since I alone suffered." "Whom do you mean, Mrs Johnson? who did you think was likely to suffer too?" "Why, madam, I am very sure Miss Grafton seeks to undermine you in her aunt's esteem. She began an artful tale to my lady, and thought to have weakened your interest; but Mrs Grafton understood not her design, and took it for granted, she meant me. Miss Grafton had the address then, by varying her plan a little, to draw me in for the whole.

"My lady, tho' one of the best of women, will yet very seldom suffer any one to defend their own cause. I begged to be allowed to clear myself of the imputation of embezzlement, but she would not see me. I sent my books to her, by Miss Grafton, she immediately returned them to me, saying, her aunt was fully convinced of my baseness, and ordered me to leave the house the next day. I had not one friend in the family to intercede for me. It is very hard, my dear young lady, after five and thirty years service to be discarded at last in my old age, with a bad name

But I hope a time will come, when I may assert my innocence. And heaven preserve you, my dear madam, from all secret enemies! Miss Grafton will never be a friend to a good person. She envies, what she cannot attain."

"You surprise me, Mrs Johnson, why should Miss Grafton be my enemy? I am sure she has no cause."

"You are too good and too handsome, my dear Miss Melmoth, to have a friend in one who looks on you as a bar to her interest."

"She sees me then in a false light. I would not be a bar to her interest for the world; on the contrary, she knows I have promoted it all in my power. Mrs Grafton was not inclined to think favourably of her, from her uncle's leaving her intirely dependent. What were Mr Melmoth's motives, I know not, but I, happily for Miss Grafton, put such a construction on it, as pleased my patroness, and made the situation of Miss Grafton much more agreeable, as you know, than first it promised to be."

"Highly as I respect my benefactress, I should be very sorry to receive any proofs of her tenderness, which would prejudice her niece. It is unjust, therefore, in Miss Grafton, to seek to deprive me of the kindness of my best friend, since she has reason, from what is past, to believe all my influence would be exerted in her favor."

I asked Mrs Johnson, how she intended to dispose of herself.

"It would be needless" said she, "to attempt getting another place, I grow old. I intend to live as well as I can, on what trifle I have remaining—A little will serve me."

I begged

I begged the poor woman's acceptance of a *note*, to make that little more. She has maintained an aged father and mother many years. They, together with an extravagant son, have kept her rather low in circumstances. I will from time to time assist her with a trifle. I requested her to remain in London, as I should then have an opportunity of serving her.

I find by Miss Grafton, the time at Bath passed not away so pleasantly as was expected. Sir George was not in his usual spirits. He complained of being fatigued, before they had been there a fortnight. Lady Darnley was not pleased with her son's inconstancy of temper, for he had been very desirous of going thither.

Could I, my dear Sidney, flatter myself, that my company was wanting, to make the place agreeable, how happy should I be!

He is gone to Wellborough, the seat of Mr. Stanhope. He set out two days before I came home. He knew I was expected; but could I expect him to wait to see me?

I have been once to see Lady Darnley; but as the young baronet was not there, the visit is not worth writing about. It would be cruel too, to pass over all the company unnoticed. Sir John Evelin was there. He did not expect to see me, he said, which may account for the confusion he appeared in, when I first spoke to him. He is an amiable man! one with whom I can converse freely, without danger to myself. Ah, would to heaven I could have secured my heart against the charms of Darnley!—Adieu, my dear Sidney.

Your's

CAROLINE MELMOTH.

LETTER

LETTER XXIV.

To EDWARD GRENVILLE, Efq,

Bruton-street, March 20

YOU condemn me, Grenville, for impofing filence on myfelf. Perhaps were I to follow your advice, and my own inclination---which ever leads to difclofe every fecret of my heart, I might lofe the bleffing I at prefent enjoy.

Mifs Melmoth frequently converfes with me; and with greater freedom than any man befide. I dread left I fhould be deprived of the pleafure I now tafte, were I to difclofe to her the fentiments of the moft faithful heart that ever woman fubdued. And yet how difficult do I find it to preferve filence.

I fometimes flatter myfelf, an offer from me would not be rejected.

My character and rank in life confidered I might reafonably expect to have a powerful advocate in Mrs Grafton, were I to folicit her intereft; but my paffion, for the lovely Caroline, is too fincere---too pure. 'Tis fhe alone muft pronounce my happinefs---or mifery. Miferable, Grenville, I fear I fhall be, if refufed by Mifs Melmoth! But if fhe allows me to call her mine,---O Grenville! there is ecftacy in the thought! Amiable, deferving maid!---Is it not folly tho', to indulge myfelf with thefe flattering ideas?

You tell me, Grenville, I am too modeft ---that my diffidence cafts a veil over my good qualities, and prevents their being confpicuous to every eye in their native luftre.---I expect not flattery from my friend, when I afk counfel,---but I will endeavour to profit by it.

I want

I want Miss Melmoth to discover my passion, by my respectful behaviour to her. But you will say, how am I to know she has made this discovery? to tell you the truth, Grenville, I believe she already has.

I went last night by accident to the play. In an opposite box sat my adorable Caroline, Miss Grafton, Mrs Cleveland, and some others. At the end of the first act, I went round to them---The box was by this time pretty well filled. I continued standing, after I had paid my compliments severally to the ladies. Miss Melmoth made room for me, between herself and Mrs Cleveland. We entered into conversation immediately. Most agreeable to me was every thing she uttered.

" Her words such a pleasure conveys,
" So much I her accents adore;
" Let her speak, and whatever she says,
" I am sure still to love her the more."

I never was so inattentive to a theatrical performance in my life, or ever half so happy. I sat gazing on her with the utmost delight. I had opportunity sufficient, as her lovely eyes were fixed on the stage.

She turned her beauteous face, to ask me some question, and discovered me in the situation I have just described. She seemed surprised, and tho' I instantaneously removed my eyes, yet a charming blush overspread her countenance. I was vexed with myself, for occasioning the least confusion in her ——You know I am not a starer, but have ever condemned those of my sex, and held them very low in my esteem, who make a practice of putting the modest part of the other out of countenance

tenance ——Tho' it muſt be owned, there are too many ladies who are in no danger of being hurt by ſuch notice, but will return ſtare for ſtare, but Miſs Melmoth differs from moſt of her ſex

After the play, ſhe moſt obligingly gave me her hand, tho' that honor was ſolicited by a number of beaux

Lord D more forward than the forwardeſt, preſt thro' the crowd in the lobby,——and ſwearing aloud " ſhe was an angel," endeavoured to wreſt the glory of conducting her to the coach from me, but ſhe, wholly diſregarding the officiouſneſs of the impertinent peer,---begged me to uſe all expedition in getting thro' the concourſe of people waiting there, adding, " I put myſelf totally under your protection "

She held up her ſack with one hand, while the other was under my arm " Have you not one hand left for me ?" aſked Lord D " I require no other conductor than Sir John Evelin," was her anſwer How happy did the diſtinction make me!

From theſe trifling incidents, Grenville, do I flatter myſelf, I am not diſagreeable to Miſs Melmoth

I will endeavour to aſſume courage to tell her I adore her Wiſh me ſucceſs,---but I know you will heaven grant it me, and the happieſt of men will be

Your

JOHN EVELIN

LETTER

LETTER XXV.

To Miss Melmoth.

Grosvenor-Square, March 25.

SIR George is returned, my dear Sidney, but I call not for your congratulations At first, indeed, I thought he seemed overjoyed to see me; but his tender behaviour soon gave place to a chilling coolness. Fool that I am, why do I weep!

How my heart fluttered, when at Lady Darnley's door, Frederic told us, he arrived that morning After so long an absence, from November to March, four long, long, tedious months, so many ages to me

Ah Sidney! why was his behaviour ever [so flatteringly] different from what it now is? and why can I not tear the self-destructive passion from my bosom?

He has lost much of his former vivacity he used, you know, to be remarkably chearful, but he is now totally changed.

I do not like that friend of his, that Stanhope They say he is a very gay man, quite a free liver Do men, I wonder, make confidents of one another, as we do? Perhaps Sir George may have acquainted Mr Stanhope with all his secrets,——for I cannot still help thinking, there was a time when I was not indifferent to him, and he [Stanhope I mean] may have represented his partiality as a ridiculous one——Friends have great influence To this journey may I owe much uneasiness Sidney, I am not well, my spirits are depress'd but I will have done with a subject, painful to me, in reciting, and from your exquisite sensibility and
tenderness

endernefs for me, equally painful for you to perufe

As the fpring promifes to be an exceeding fine one, Mr. Grafton intends going very early this year to Melmoth-Caftle.

The fteward writes her, the alterations are juft finifhed. She is impatient to be at the place of her nativity. What happy days have I paffed there in my infancy! May they return! but I much fear they never will to

Your

CAROLINE MELMOTH

LETTER XXVI.

To Mifs VERE.

Grofvenor-Square, March 28.

I Am almoft afhamed to acquaint my deareft Sidney with the ridiculous weaknefs of her friend. I am difpleafed with every thing I do or fay; how vain then to hope to pleafe others, when, notwithftanding the natural affection we bear ourfelves, we are not fatisfied with our own proceedings.

Laft night Sir John Evelin was here; he fat by me great part of the evening. I happened to be [very wonderful!] in rather a talkative mood; he paid polite attention to my chat, but appeared at times very thoughtful and melancholy. He feemed feveral times as if he was going to utter fomething, but checked himfelf. He did not ftay fupper, Sir George Darnley and his fifter did. Sir
George's

George's behaviour, I thought, was particular to Mi's Grafton—he took very little notice of your Caroline—

A few crofs incidents concurred to render the night a fleeplefs one to me—

This morning Sir John Evelin called again. Mifs Grafton was paying vifits, and Mrs Grafton was confined in her room by a cold—I went into the parlour to receive him. You know, when with you, I hinted my fufpicions that Sir John entertained a partiality for me, which I was forry for—

We entered into an indifferent converfation,——but fo conftrained, on his part, that a fitter by, without much penetration, might have difcovered he laboured under fome anxiety of mind. He frequently paufed,—fighed,—and refumed a topic that could not give rife to a figh—

At laft he fpoke of Mr Grafton-Melmoth, mentioned him with the warmeft affection, and fincerely lamented his death—

" I wonder not," faid he, " my friend fhould fo much regret the lofs of life, fince, in lofing his exiftence, he likewife loft the hope of being united to the moft lovely and amiable woman in the world. The only confolation muft be, his not knowing all your perfections—Had he feen you, as I behold you "—he paufed, fighed, and looked down, then refuming his difcourfe, " Pardon me, madam, that I have thus avowed a flame, which but received addition from the fight of your perfon. Prepared to admire, from the praifes my friend beftowed on you, I made it my bufinefs to get introduced to Mrs Grafton—My intimacy with her late amiable nephew, rendered it eafy—You were then abfent on a vifit at Vere-Park—

" I found

"I found Miss Grafton's person agreeable, what many people think handsome. Since I have been capable of judging of the happiness which must accrue from an union of hearts, I have wished to meet with a woman, in whose society I could hope to find true felicity. I have therefore, beheld the fair sex, with rather an eye of scrutiny. I very soon became certain Miss Grafton was not the person I was in search of.

"Every time I came hither, I wished to see the woman, who in her tender years could so far engage the heart of my sensible friend, as to induce him to request his uncle not to dispose of her, 'till his return from his travels.

"I felt myself chagrined, when your return to town was postponed. Miss Grafton did all in her power to dissipate a gloom which would sometimes, I knew not why, overspread my countenance. I was obliged to her, but the assiduity of some people does not please.

"My mother requested my presence at the Abbey. my affairs rendered it necessary, but an involuntary impulse obliged me to stay. I could not repel the inclination, or curiosity, as I then called it, I had to see you.

"One day I entered Mrs Grafton's drawing room. My heart, which had been ever free from the emotions of love, ceased to be so the moment I fixed my eyes on the most lovely object I ever beheld. In vain I turned them to other ladies, with whom the room was filled, they involuntarily strayed to her. A sentiment I never experienced before, took possession of my soul. I could scarcely believe it possible any one at first sight could have had such an effect upon me. In an instant, I became sensible of the power of beauty. I used to ridicule those who lost their hearts to a fair face. Is it possible, said I to myself, a lovely person alone can raise these emotions in my breast? Again I gazed on that heavenly face, and beheld every virtue, every grace depicted there. Wisdom, modesty, and honor, gave embellishment to the finest set of features in the world.

"Lost in rapture, I remained ardently gazing, while the beautiful object seemed alone unknowing of her charms, or the effect they had on the beholders.

"Miss Grafton perceived me, and coming up to me, in order to divert my attention from the angelic creature, which engrossed my every faculty, desired me to take a seat at the card-table; I begged to be excused; but engaged her in conversation, and in as careless an air as I could assume, I asked who that lady was. Ah! how my heart bounded! how every nerve vibrated the name of Miss Melmoth.

"If the view of your charms alone, had such an effect, how was that effect augmented in the short time I was so happy as to converse with you! Your conquest was then complete. My reason approved my passion, my judgment confirmed my choice. And, oh! that I might hope you would not condemn it," continued he, raising his eyes to mine, and taking my hand; " that you would allow me to hope that time, and my faithful assiduity, may render me in the least worthy a return,———then would you behold me the happiest of men."

Can you account for it, my Sidney?—I cannot: unless by saying, my spirits have for some time been very low, and all the time Sir John was speaking, my idea was wholly filled by another object. I sighed, and wished to myself, that it was

the

the too amiable Darnley, who was making the offer. His image swam before my eyes.

Sir John continued, "Say, my ever amiable Mrs Melmoth, may the man before you hope, he is not difagreeable to you? Will you accept his whole services? Will you, lovely and best beloved of women, deign to bless the most faithful of men?"—He stopped, as if to give me time to answer him.

Ah Sidney! I am amazed at my folly. I held down my head——I remained silent. My bosom heaved with sighs. Tears gushed from my brimful eyes, and fell in fast drops down my cheeks. What could Sir John think? What interpretation give to my emotions?

"Heavens!" exclaimed he, quitting my hand, which I had not the recollection to withdraw, so lost was I in painful cogitation,——with a look of the utmost surprise, mingled with concern, "What mean these tears?——these sighs?" Then rising and turning from me, his eyes bent on the floor—— "Their meaning is, alas! too obvious unhappy, ill-fated Evelin!"

I endeavoured to speak. "Ah, spare me, spare me, the cruel truth," interrupted Sir John. "Pardon, Madam, and, if possible, do not hate the man, whose presumptuous hopes have rendered him for ever miserable"——He was going speech was lent me. "Stay, Sir John, stay, and do not leave me thus. Ah! could you see my heart,—and yet perhaps you would despise me.—Your noble, generous and disinterested behaviour to me, deserves all the return in my power to bestow.—That power, alas! is limited, yet as far as it can extend, 'tis yours. Ah! say, can you be contented with my friendship, my esteem?—

They

They muſt, they ever have been your's —" But" continued I, ſighing, " My heart tells me, there is a ſentiment warmer than friendſhip and eſteem I find it not impoſſible to feel a tender lively eſteem for you, even while my heart is under the influence of a leſs ſerene paſſion

" It is to you, and you alone, I would avow theſe ſentiments, which are the genuine ones of a heart incapable of deceit, and which never gives pain to any one, without doubly feeling it itſelf how ſenſibly then muſt I ſympathize in the diſtreſs of a man, to whoſe friendſhip I would wiſh to aſpire? Suffer me," taking his hand,——" to ſolicit yours, in return for mine.——Permit me to behold you in the light of a ſincere amiable friend and brother "———I ſtopped

While I had been ſpeaking, he continued ſilent, his eyes fixed on the ground, and now and then a ſigh eſcaped him, which pierced my heart· at length, turning towards me, and gently preſſing my hand, " Since," ſaid he, in a broken voice, " your friendſhip is all I dare hope for, with joy I accept it And," bending his knee, " here I ſwear to dedicate my whole life to that alone never ſhall my heart own the power of any other, or ſhall my tongue offend you by a repetition of my paſſion Yes, moſt adorable Caroline," raiſing my hand to his lips, " friendſh p alone, friendſhip heightened by tenderneſs, ſhall fill my ſoul. May you be happy, where you have fixed your choice! And oh! may the man, moſt happy, be worthy of your love!——May his paſſion equal mine!"—He ſpoke the laſt words with great difficulty,——tears ſtarted from his eyes, and the effort he made to conceal his tender ſenſibility almoſt overcame him.——I wept.———He aroſe.

" But, as an aggravation to my woe, I am afraid the

the most deserving of her sex is not happy Ah! these tears are not an indication of a heart at rest speak, my dear Miss Melmoth, say, is it in the power of your friend to assist you? Perhaps want of fortune may be the obstacle?———if that be the case, make no difficulty of accepting part of mine ———it is no compliment to offer that to you, which is of no use to myself The possession of millions can never give ease to my heart, but if parting with half my estate can render you happy with the man you love, take,———command it while I will remain content with the share of felicity, which will accrue to me from seeing you blest"

Ah! Sidney, what a heart has this man! I made him my most grateful acknowledgements,—but could I find proper words to express my sense of his merit '———no words were too weak One continued obligation as my life has ever been, I never till this moment felt so much the want of power to return them there is but one way,——— at least my heart could suggest no other,———which was to endeavour to suppress his ill-placed passion ————He was too generous to hint a desire of knowing for whom I sighed, only repeated his offer of all in his power to effect my felicity

I told him, " I feared I was unworthy his esteem Ah!" said I, " would you not despise the woman who could suffer her heart to entertain more than esteem for a man, who is not only insensible of her passion, but, I fear, owns another flame? I condemn myself every moment of my life, but cannot even endeavour to eradicate a tenderness which seems part of myself. I plainly see my folly, yet cannot resolve to relinquish it I have not the slightest prospect of hope, yet ought I not to blush to own it? I love fervently,——— ardently love"

" And

"And you muſt be beloved again," ſaid Sir John, "it is impoſſible any man can long remain inſenſible of your tenderneſs Ah, that I had influence over him!---That he beheld you with my eyes! Then ſhould I ſoon hear of your being happy It would be long ere I could truſt myſelf to be eye-witneſs of it Heaven grant you may be ſoon happy with the worthieſt of men!------worthy I am ſure he muſt be, to be diſtinguiſhed by you."

He ſtrove to aſſume an eaſy air; but a leſs diſcerning eye muſt have diſcovered his ſufferings. He ſeemed going to ſay ſomething more, but checked himſelf. He bowed, ſighed,---turned haſtily from me, and hurried out of the room

Ah, may he ſoon recover his loſt peace of mind! How ſincerely do I pity him! Do I not too well know what are his ſufferings? A hopeleſs paſſion! O my God, what pangs does that heart endure, which is a prey to a hopeleſs paſſion,---the worſt of ills!

Ah! why are our hearts formed with ſuch tender ſenſibility? Why ſo ſuſceptible of love?--- Why ſo apt to receive the fatal impreſſion,---ſo incapable of inſpiring a mutual paſſion? My grief is all renewed: I have done nothing but weep ſince morning Ah! why can I not do juſtice to the merit of Sir John Evelyn? I cannot,---I feel, I cannot I admire, I revere his many excellencies,---a heart firmly attached to another, can do no more,---that other too, likewiſe worthy Ah, Sidney! too eminently ſo for me!

Could I vainly hope he would for me diſappoint the hopes of his family?---Yet the Evelyns boaſt a deſcent as high as the Darnleys

Whenever I go to St. James's-ſquare Sir George finds ſome pretence to leave us. ---a pretence I
fear

fear it is. I am not pleasing to his sight, but surely I am not an object of disgust! Yet his behaviour is so different to what it used to be,—so very different to every body else, so much constrained civility. Sometimes I am apt to think I have done something to displease him. I have not variety enough in my character; my ready acquiescence to the will of others, may be termed insipidity.

Thus, by striving to please, I have defeated my own purpose. I know not what to think; but I am unhappy. Ah, that I may ever be otherwise!

Adieu, my dearest Sidney; believe me

Your's for ever,

Caroline Melmoth.

LETTER XXVII.

To Miss Vere.

Grosvenor Square, April 2.

THIS is the last letter you will receive from me 'till I arrive at the Castle. Mrs. Grafton proposes setting out the beginning of next week. My heart feels very heavy on the occasion. I shall be so much farther removed from my Sidney; so much longer will it be before I receive her dear letters,——my chief solace.

Mrs Grafton invited Sir John Evelin to be of our party, saying she would engage some more company (the Darnley family she meant) to induce him to give us his. He looked at me with great significance, and very politely declined accepting

her

her offer, alledging an indispensable obligation to be with a friend who was going to the Spa——I believe his excuse was premature

Mrs Grafton asked him how long it would be, before he left England?---Naming a time at some distance, she would take no denial, " he must spend a few days at Melmoth-Castle "-—-Miss Grafton joined her entreaties it would have looked particular in me, had I been silent His eyes glistened when I made my request, and for some moments, his whole countenance wore the trace of joy,——which, however, too soon gave way to a melancholy languor

How distressing to a heart tender as mine, to behold so worthy a man unhappy!——To know myself the cause---But is my situation less perplexing than his? He knows I pity him Have I that consolation? Ah, no!

Having an opportunity, I asked Sir John who the friend was with whom he was going to the Spa, his blush and down-cast eye confirmed me in my first conjecture

After remaining some time silent, he cast a melancholy glance on me, and deeply sighing, said, " The man, my ever amiable Miss Melmoth, who flatters himself, he can possibly say to his affections, Thus far you shall go, and no farther, when wholly engrossed by a truly deserving object, will find himself deceived, as I have been I vainly hoped, from the pleasure I experienced, when you promised me your friendship, I could have remained satisfied with that alone, but I find my heart refractory I cannot behold you without admiration, —an admiration too tender for friendship, nor can I restrain my eyes and tongue from disclosing the feelings of my heart It is therefore highly necessary I should quit your presence I ought not to have

have suffered myself to be persuaded to accompany you to the Castle with what foundation can I hope to conquer a passion displeasing to you, if I cannot even keep the resolution I had formed of flying from you How dearly do I pay, for thus indulging myself! I am miserable, but have not the wretch's consolation——the privilege of complaint ——of whom should I complain? of you?——surely not you pity me Ah! learn, my rebellious heart, to be grateful for the only blessing thou enjoyest, the pity of the most amiable of women!"

How much did his apostrophe affect me! tears stood in my eyes Indeed, I felt his sufferings I could only utter my sincere wish of his finding all the benefit he merited Hoped he would soon be able to return, as I should ever regret the absence (more the occasion of it) of so amiable a friend"

April 3.

Mrs Grafton has, I find, according to her promise, engaged the Darnley-family to be of our party She says, she will do all in her power to make us merry and happy ——Merry and happy! What different meanings have those two words! What different ideas of the last we all have! Equally in search of the phantom happiness, how various our pursuits; and, ah! how fruitless they prove!

I really think Mr Lumley the happiest man in the world, as his felicity is to be purchased, and he has a fine fortune to supply himself with articles of happiness

What joy have I seen in his eager face, when he has made any acquisition to his collection of antiques!

You can't imagine what favor I am in with the old virtuoso, for accidentally, as you may suppose, giving the preference to an old broken bronze,
which

which was treated with neglect by some of the company. He applauded my just taste to the fifth heaven, and swore [tremendous oath!] by the foot of Pharoah, I had the true original gusto

Nay, he was absolutely going to make a comparison between my face and a bust of the famed Cleopatra, which he assured me, upon his veracity, would be to my advantage, as I had a certain softness, which the fair Egyptian could make no pretensions to. Is not the fair Egyptian an odd epithet? I am rather apt to substitute that of brown

He told Sir George, with a very profound air, he thought me one of the finest moderns he had ever viewed, " lamented the depraved barbarism of the times, which would consign so fine a figure to the earth, instead of preserving the body intire, to create the admiration of succeeding ages "

I had enough to do to prevent laughing in old Periwinkle's face. Only form an idea of a man contemplating the figure a fine young woman will make when she is dead, and anticipating with pleasure the beauty of her bones divested of their covering

Sir George said, I should make a very pretty addition to Mr Lumley's collection of natural curiosities

" Miss Melmoth would be at the head of my moderns, I assure you, Sir George. Come a little more this way, Madam.—Don't you perceive, Sir George, a very great similarity in the turn of Miss Melmoth's neck, with that Grecian Venus over the door?——We have not an opportunity of carrying the comparison farther, as the young lady has, by an useless incumbrance, deprived us of beholding beauties which nature meant not to hide "

You may figure to yourself what was my situation the while. I colored, as well thro' shame his vexation. Sir George seemed to enjoy my distress, and augmented it by saying, he hoped my husband would be a man of virtue, and communicative likewise, he then might oblige the world with his discoveries and observations.

"Few men, replied the virtuoso, have genius requisite for such observations. Men are too apt to take a woman tout ensemble. Now for my part, when I am told such and such are fine women, I examine them closely, not by the common rule of judgment, which is frequently erroneous, but by those known only to the philosophic world which is, I presume, the reason I can so seldom pronounce a woman perfect,—in her person I mean. For instance, there is lady S—— B——. Her nose is the nineteenth part of an inch too acquiline. Lady W——'s mouth is, according to the true and only criterion of personal perfection, about the same proportion too wide, and yet these ladies are toasts.

"There is Mrs ——, now Lady A. She is esteemed very handsome by most people. But any one, whose eyes have been accustomed to contemplate the Venus de Medicis, must be disgusted with the preposterous size of her head. Indeed I believe, it is not altogether a natural infirmity, I have been told, I know not with what certainty, that she is indebted to art for the magnitude of her capitol. But is it not amazing, Sir George, that a woman born beautiful, should endeavour to subvert that, to most a desirable acquisition, and render herself, at least to a true connoisseur, not a pleasing object of meditation?"

How much longer he would have proceeded, I know not, but luckily his attention was called off, by Miss Grafton's having accidentally brushed down with her hoop a glass,—a frightful old-fashioned thing,

thing, with a piece knocked off the bottom. He was in a moſt dreadful agony, leſt it ſhould have ſuſtained further damage. He carefully took it up; and to his inexpreſſible joy, found it came off pretty well, that is, only with the loſs of a piece more from the foot.

I expreſſed ſome ſurpriſe at his diſtreſs, which he "aſſured me would ceaſe, when he informed me it was the very identical glaſs, in which Rowena, the daughter of Hengiſt, drank the firſt health to Vortigern. it is true," added he, " it is not very antique, and I have ſeveral things infinitely more curious, but the extreme difficulty I had in procuring it—it coſt me fifteen years in reſcuing it from the obſcurity which the tumult of thoſe times had condemned it to—and there being only this in the world—ſtamps an indelible value on it."

We left the old philoſopher very buſy in replacing ſome things, which we had, to oblige him, inſpected with much ſeeming ſatisfaction, tho' with very little real pleaſure—at leaſt, I can anſwer for myſelf, I was heartily fatigued.

We ſhall make quite a grand cavalcade to the caſtle.

Lord and Lady P will honor us with their company for a few days.—Her brother, Lord William B too. You know him, I believe: a very amiable young man. He has not yet recovered the melancholy, into which the death of his lovely wife, about a year ago, threw him. Her death was attended with very affecting circumſtances. Lady P could hardly perſuade him to go with us, he was ſo unwilling to leave his little daughter, whoſe birth commenced as the laſt breath departed from her mother. The manner of her diſſolution often brings to my mind, that beautiful old ballad of the birth of Saint George. You are, I know a very

great

great admirer of ancient poetry, and would pardon my quoting some of those lines; but it would be needless, as you may turn to it, and read the whole.

Lord L drank tea here this afternoon; and felt invited attends us. The rest of our party you are acquainted with. Ah, that my Sidney was to make one! out of all these, I cannot select one, with whom I can use unlimited confidence; in whose bosom save yours, can I repose my griefs? The Miss Darnley's I love exceedingly, but they are excluded. Miss Grafton, for the same reason —Again I repeat, would to heaven you were here! but this wish is as vain as mine generally are.

Miss Grafton plumes herself [Harriot's phrase that] on Sir John Evelin's accompanying us. She said, with some pleasure, I thought, had she not joined her intreaties, he would not have been prevailed on to go. She is very happy, no doubt, in his affections. I wish her surmises were with any foundation. She builds much upon the same basis as myself, I believe.

I can indulge myself no longer in scribbling to you, as I have a thousand things to do, which must be dispatched with great alacrity. My time is but short; and I must bestow half an hour on poor Mrs Johnson. How I wish I could re-instate her in Mrs Grafton's favor! My dear patroness would be more than woman, was it not for that little shade in her character. I thank you, my dear girl, for the present you sent the poor woman; you have highly obliged me in it.

Let me have the pleasure of hearing from you soon, your last letter bears a long date. you mentioned nothing of Miss Arnold in it, present my compliments to her.

Believe me your's, with the truest affection.
CAROLINE MELMOTH.

LETTER XXVIII.

To Miss Melmoth.

Vere-Park, April 6.

YOUR reproof is just, my dear, indeed I have been long in your debt.

I am not so well pleased with Miss Arnold as I thought I should have been. But I will acquaint you with my reasons, lest you think it proceeds from a natural fickleness in your Sidney.

You may remember my once writing to you of Miss Arnold's complaining, Robert the butler did not pay her proper respect,* and likewise, that he was discharged on that account. We hired one in his room, with whom we had a written character.

A few days since, I went to pay a visit, Miss Arnold excused herself from accompanying me. Finding the lady rather indisposed, I made it a very short one; the evening being very fine, I proposed undressing myself, and taking a walk. In passing thro' the gallery at the end of the lobby, I heard William's voice, [the new servant,] talking in a very jocose manner in the anti-chamber adjoining my dressing-room, and Miss Arnold laughing heartily. I stopt thro' surprise. They proceeded in their mirth. I then stepped into the library, and rung the bell. Nobody appearing, I rang it again, pretty smartly. 〈…〉 up the front staircase,

〈…〉 old." "Miss Arnold—madam?" "Yes. I suppose you will have no difficulty in finding her, since you left her this instant in my

* Which letter did not appear.

my anti-chamber" He looked a good deal confused, and left the room

You will perhaps accuse me, my love, of speaking very petulantly to the servant I do not make a practice of it, but I was vexed

Miss Arnold made her appearance and with an affected air of surprise, "Dear madam, I did not know you was returned so soon. What are your commands with me?"

"I wanted your company in a walk, if you are not engaged" "Engaged!" with a conscious earnestness, "what engagement can she have, whose all she owes to your bounty?"

"You seemed deeply engaged just now with William I could not have supposed it was for that reason you refused attending me on my visit,—or that you would so far have degenerated from yourself, as to behave with such familiarity with a servant, which ever, in people of their class, breeds contempt No wonder Robert lost sight of his respect for you, if is is your method to make domestics your companions We must pay a proper deference to ourselves if we expect to receive it from our inferiors"

"Ah! my dear madam," said she, shedding tears, "you no longer behold me with the eyes you used to do my every action now displeases my benefactress"

"I am sure, dear Lucy, you have no reason to say so" "Have I not, madam, when you are so ready to misconstrue an action wholly innocent, and I may say laudable?

"From the first of my seeing William I thought his person no stranger to me, tho' I could never recollect, when, or where, I had seen him. This afternoon, when he brought me my tea, I told him, I was certain I had seen him before Very likely,

likely, madam, he anfwered, for I have feen you, I am fure Of what country are you? Gloucefter-fhire, madam Upon further inquiry, I found, he was born in a village three miles from the town I lived in I could not reftrain my curiofity from afking a few queftions relative to my native place, It is natural, madam, to have a partiality for a place where we firft drew breath, and paffed our infant years

"I afked him feveral queftions He gave me fuch a droll account of the wedding of a fatirical old maid, that I could not forbear laughing with him I fhall never repeat any converfation with him again—or indeed, fhall I have occafion, as he informed me of all I wanted to know"

Now do you know, my dear Caroline, I do not implicitly believe all Mifs Arnold fays The ftory does not hold together very cleverly I think, were I in her fituation, I fhould have been defirous of remaining concealed from the knowledge of every one, particularly a fervant If this fellow lived within three miles of the town, he muft have heard of Mr Arnold's family, and likewife the ftory of her misfortunes, which fhe owns was very well known,—and told with circumftances injurious to her reputation Befides, how could he inform her of this wedding, with fuch circumftances attending it, as to excite fo much laughter, when his character fays, he lived in his laft place three years, and left it immediately as he came to us?

All thefe things put together, have leffened my opinion of Mifs Arnold, and of my own judgment in fome meafure She feems to have fo much art. And then her tears are always ready to flow in an inftant In fhort, I am not half fatisfied with her. however, I will endeavour to foil her at her own weapon

F 4 My

My father is grown prodigiously fond of her I promised myself an agreeable companion in her, but she is now very seldom with me; generally excusing herself, when I go out.

She very readily joins now in all conversations and has lost most of that pleasing diffidence and humility, which I used to admire in her so much. She sometimes seems to have a perfect knowledge of some things, which I should not suppose a girl never in London could be acquainted with.

You know, when you was down with us, my father scarce took any notice of her, which vexed me exceedingly; but now the case is altered quite, he extols what she says, upon every occasion, as if she spoke with the eloquence of Cicero. says, she has a very fine understanding, conspicuous in the most agreeable choice of words he ever met with in a woman. This he said before her. I made answer, "Yes, she could tell a story very well." I was a little piqued with my father, which perhaps gave an emphasis to the words, as might make them alarming, at least, they appeared so to Miss Arnold, for she was greatly confounded, tho' she had the address to seem only so, by my father's praises. I am convinced, she must have been an imprudent girl.

But enough of this dull subject. If I find I am not better pleased with her soon, I shall contrive some way to part with her.

I pity poor Evelin with all my soul, and wish he may recover his heart, since you are determined to be cruel. He is a charming fellow. Pity his tender blossom of love should be blighted. Cannot you transfer him now to a friend? not you. I'll warrant. Letty shall not have him, that's poz.

You shall hear from me again soon. I will therefore say not a word of Darnley, only wish
you

you loved him less, or he shewed more affection for you. I know not what to make of him, but am apt to think as you do, that Stanhope does him no good.

Adieu, my dearest Caroline. None of your fellows can exceed, in true affection,

Your

SIDNEY VERE.

LETTER XXIX

To Miss VERE

Melmoth-Castle, April 23.

I Began a letter on my first coming hither, but had not an opportunity of finishing it, as my days were sufficiently employed with helping to entertain our guests, and my nights were not my own, as Miss Grafton slept with me, we being rather straitened for room (part of the castle being still unfurnished) for like a snow-ball, we gathered in our journey, and, to carry on the metaphor, we are all melted away again.

Concerts, balls, and excursions, round the country, helped to wear away the day without answering any other purpose.

We all came hither with an intent to be happy but as every one had not used the precaution of leaving their cares behind them, some would now and then intrude, and convinced us, notwithstanding we racked our minds, and fatigued our bodies, to procure happiness, something would still interfere, to render it incomplete.

If I speak my mind freely, the only one of the company, who approached nearest the goal we were all striving to reach, was the young countess of P who was inceffantly complaining, and lamenting fome misfortune or other Strange you will fay, fure you miftake No, my dear; a little infpection into the character of the countess will unravel this feeming paradox her evils, were always evils of the day or hour Had she not been uncommonly fortunate in her journey through life, she could not fo emphatically have lamented a shower of rain, which for half an hour prevented her whimfical ladyship from going to fee the fifh leap in the great canal Muft not the heart be unacquainted with any kind of diftrefs, that can be difcompofed by fuch trifles?

Sir John Evelin ftaid a week only with us Mr Grenville, his intimate friend, called on him, and took him from us

Mr Grenville is to Sir John Evelin, what my beloved Sidney is to me, a kind, indulgent, tender, inftructive friend

" There are few,' faid Sir John, " we can efteem as few likewife we would wifh fhould efteem us I muft endeavour to conciliate as much as in me l es, the friendfhip of thofe few I love Yourfelf and mr Grenville fhare my whole heart —no rivals fhall you ever have "

One day Sir Ceorge was expatiating on the beauty of the Spa Mifs Grafton cautioned Sr John againft the beauty of the inhabitants, " as it would be paying dear," faid fhe, " if from complaifance to your friend, you fhould lofe your heart "

I cannot think there will be any danger," returned Sir John if a man can live unmoved in fuch fociety," bowing to the ladies, " he may

moft

most likely escape the snares of foreign beauties: and if his heart is filled with the lovely image of one of his fair country-women, he will be more secure still."

"We speak highly, and most justly," said Sir George, "of the beauty of our ladies; but tho' I must in general give them the preference, I by no means exclude those of other nations. In every country I have visited, I have seen very lovely women. One I particularly remember, a Neapolitan I think, for the exterior, I never saw her equal, in all my travels. I could not behold her without thinking of Richardson's Clementina. I was not singular in my admiration of her; for I believe there was scarce any foreigner of figure, who did not attempt to be introduced to the "Bella Signiora," as she was called, by way of eminence."

"And had you the happiness, brother," asked Harriot, "to"———"Be introduced, do you mean? I had. And no small happiness I thought it, Harriot, tho' her charms proved fatal to many."

Ah! Sidney, perhaps they proved fatal to him too. May not this be the lady,—the beautiful Italian that Louisa spoke of, from a hint Lord Wilton threw out?—He spoke warmly. Ah! should it be so! Tormenting idea!

The morning after Mr Grenville arrived, Sir John took leave of us. I re-assured him he had the second place in my heart. He repeated his tender and sincere wishes for my happiness,—and with great emotion bade me farewel.

I was affected with his honest sensibility. I re-tired to my room, and gave a free discharge from my over-loaded heart.

This

This abominable love is " the difturber of high and of low." I pleafed myfelf in having fo amiable a man, with whom I could converfe freely, and without danger, for my friend: but I am difappointed. From my firft acquaintance with Sir John, I felt a great partiality for him, which perhaps, had I never known Darnley, might in time have proved a more tender fentiment: but that is now intirely out of the queftion. I have no heart to reward his merit.—I never can love but one,—or ceafe to love that one. I am convinced my heart was formed to receive one fixed and conftant paffion, ard Darnley, the amiable Darnley, to excite it.

Well as I faid before, " our guefts are departed, and their kiffes forgot." I can't honeftly fay all tho', but no matter.

I think it was rather impolitic of Mrs. Grafton, to have fo much company down at one time, as they, with œconomy, might have lafted beft part of the fummer. We feem fo filent now,——fo much alone. I have, it is true, the freer ufe of my time and thoughts, and may communicate them to you: but are they pleafing thoughts? by no means.

Tired with reflections, I fometimes take up a book, but I read with a divided attention. if the fubject is pleafant, I figh becaufe I cannot enjoy it, if melancholy, I draw fo many inferences, and make fo many applications, that I am not able to go on. I lofe all relifh for my moft favorite avocations. Mufic melts me,—I cannot work long together,—in fhort, I am fit for nothing. Ah! how different are the prefent, from thofe days when we ufed alternately to work and read? Happy, peaceful, gentle hours, ever to be regretted, ye are paft! never, I fear, to return to me!

I am

I am very much concerned at your having any cause for not being satisfied with Miss Arnold's behaviour. You should not condemn her, my beloved Sidney, for being innocently chearful. Consider, my dear, in how narrow a circle must all her comforts lie. Deny her not what you can afford her. Can all the enjoyments of this life render her happy? No. Then be not angry with poor Miss Arnold, if she for a moment ceases to mourn her truly hapless fate. Better overlook what is passed. You seem chagrined at your father's notice of her; don't let me have cause to think my Sidney capricious. did you not wish your father might approve your conduct to the fair unfortunate, and will you be displeased, when that event has taken place?

I will not say a word more, in answer to your letter. some part of it pained me, but your conclusion was a cordial to

Your ever grateful

CAROLINE MELMOTH.

Some letters betwéen Miss Melmoth and her friends, are omitted, as not being necessary to be inserted.

LETTER XXX.

TO MISS VERE.

Grosvenor-Square, May 29.

YOU find my dearest Sidney, by the date, I attended Mrs. Grafton to town, where the prosecution of her business will detain her for some

some time. I would, with the utmost pleasure, devote my time to her; but as Lady Darnley has so earnestly desired my company to the Grove, my kind patroness insists on my compliance. You will perhaps wonder at my making any objection, but abstracted from the pleasure I find in the society of my dear Mrs Grafton, I really feel myself too unhappy to wish to be exposed to the company and charms of a man, who is too, too amiable. Why, ah! why, my dear Sidney, should I subject myself to fresh temptations? Surely I have suffered enough from disappointments already.

I have seen this dear disturber of my rest twice since I came to town. But he invited me not; or if he did, it was so cool a request, I spared myself the mortification of attending to it.

To-morrow sevennight we set off. I will write to you when I arrive at Darnley-Grove; 'till then, my amiable Sidney, adieu.

CAROLINE MELMOTH.

LETTER XXXI.

To Miss VERE.

Darnley-Grove, June 18.

I Wish I had not come hither. O Sidney I am more unhappy than ever. I again repeat, I wish I had not come. What can be the meaning of Sir George Darnley's unaccountable behaviour? Surely he might be civil, if he can feel no more. What have I done to merit the slights he shews me? Does he see my partiality, and takes this method to crush my aspiring hopes? Cruel Darnley, you need not take these pains, my death, I hope, will soon prevent you. Ah! what avails

the

the uncommon kindness with which his mother and fisters treat me?———'tis nothing, while he is so cold

For a few days his behaviour was tolerable; that is, as polite and attentive as to any other indifferent person, but it has changed very much lately. I cannot imagine why I am thus to be distinguished. I was excessively piqued yesterday at something he said, so much so, that I could hardly restrain my tears 'till I reached my chamber. I summoned all my pride, and resolved he should have cause to triumph thus over me no more. I wanted to find some pretence for leaving the family. I wish I could form any scheme, which would not give rise to suspicions of the real cause, but I am a dreadful plotter.

All the rest of the day, I endeavoured to appear as unconcerned as possible,—nay, attempted to be gay. I took no notice of Sir George. I followed the same rule to-day, but my heart reproaches me, as if I was cruel to myself, in appearing neglectful of him.

How happy you ought to think yourself, my dearest Sidney! you know none of these cruel pains and anxieties which rend the heart of your friend, yet how kindly do you sympathize with me in my distresses! May your breast ever be a stranger to this destructive passion! and if ever you love, grant Heaven you may meet a reciprocal return!

My letters are ever the same. I believe I must give over writing to you, the perusal of my follies must be irksome to a heart like yours, which feels the anguish, but cannot prescribe a cure. Write to me, however, speedily, and forgive all the errors of

Your ever faithful
CAROLINE MELMOTH.
LETTER

LETTER XXXII.

To Miss VERE.

Darnley-Grove, June 26.

WHY will you endeavour to make me believe, what, alas! can never be true? You say, you are convinced Sir George Darnley is not insensible to my charms; but is he touched with them? He may allow me to be handsome and amiable, but does he love me for being so? He struggle with a concealed passion! Is it thus you mean to cure me, Sidney? Ah! cease thy siren-voice, nor lure me to my ruin.

You tell me I am too good, a little dash of the coquet would add to my charms, by shewing them, and by that means increase my conquests. I do not want to increase my conquests, were I queen of the world, I would not wish to be beloved by more than one, and that one should be Darnley.

But would you really wish me, my dearest Sidney, to follow the advice you have given me, in the letter * now before me? Is it as safe as you say it is?——I protest I am afraid to try. I am sure, yet, I have done nothing to forfeit the esteem, if ever I possessed it, of Sir George Darnley. But will he not despise me in the character of a coquet? The motive, should he discover it, would not that be still worse? You will answer for the consequences: ah, Sidney! who knows what they may be!

However, I shall pay you a greater compliment in following your advice, as it is not absolutely

consonant

---

* Miss Vere's letter does not appear.

MISS MELMOTH

consonant with my mode of thinking, that if it thoroughly coincided with my opinion, and I so seldom think right, if we judge from conclusions, that I am the more ready to make you this sacrifice besides, amidst all my follies, I have never had the consolation, if any can be found in it, of being able to blame any body but myself

An opportunity will present itself this afternoon of obeying your injunctions you have a much higher opinion of my person than I have, if you think, as you say, that admiration waits my steps, I believe no such thing, but however, will take some pains to decorate myself for D———— assembly, which is to-night. Besides it will be necessary, as I am sure I shall have a partner to seek, if I should be inclined to dance. Adieu, 'till my return

* * *

Four o'clock

Late—or rather early—as it is, I must sit down, to give you some account of the preceding evening. For what purpose should I go to bed, as Jaffier says, I have neither " rest in my eyes, or comfort in my heart ?"

Dare I own to you, I took more than common pains in dressing? which I believe was attended with success, my motive, not to enlarge my conquests, but, if possible, to atchieve impossibilities, for such, I fear, is the attaching the too-amiable Darnley to me Well, but to my dress, &c I put on a white lutestring negligèe, trimmed with a narrow gold edging, sleeve-knots and stomacher gold blond My hair, without powder, I ornamented with a little puffed lappet on one side A few diamonds well enough disposed among the back curls

curls diamond ear-rings, crofs, and fo forth. Pofitively I never looked half fo well in my eye, and yet you know a woman generally has a quick fight in thofe matters.

When dreffed, I went into Mifs Darnley's room, where I found her making fome alteration in Harriot's head-drefs, her own being ftill in difordr. " What have you two idle creatures been about, faid I, " not to be ready? I was really afraid I fhould have made you wait "

" Deuce take my head," faid Harriot, I have been tiffing it to no manner of purpofe, I can make nothing of it—Lord, look at Caroline, fee how fhe is dreffed!"

" Why, what's amifs?" afked I, fmiling

" Amifs!" fhe returned, " it is the ftrongeft proof of my good-nature I can give, that I don't tear your head-gear out of envy Look, Louifa, did you ever fee a more charming girl?"

" Pfhaw!" exclaimed I, " I am fure you don't mean what you fay, I apprehend you obferve fome impropriety in my drefs, and are rallying me upon it " " Peace, you little enchanting wretch," interrupted Harriot: " you are prepared to eclipfe us to-night, I fee, and if we treat you with the leaft degree of clemency, it is becaufe we do not expect to meet our favorite fwains "

" Pofitively," faid Mifs Darnley, " if I was not pretty certain Sir George had other thoughts I fhould be fearful for his heart ," [other thoughts mind that, Sidney ·] for could he fail falling a victim to fuch charms?"

" There feems no great danger," faid I, rather nettled at her manner of fpeaking

" Thank God," faid Harriot, " he feems bleffed in a happy indifference, or his heart is engaged.

gaged; but he is so reserved upon the subject he says we girls are so fond of, there is no forming a right judgment of his inclinations. I am apt to think though, notwithstanding his insinuations to the contrary some time ago, he has left his heart in the hands of some fair foreigner."

"How does that appear?" asked your simple friend, rather hesitatingly. "Why, my only reason," answered she, "for judging so is this," taking my hand, and leading to the glass, "View that form." "It gives me no pleasure," said I, turning away.

"Don't tell stories, Caroline. No woman upon earth, be she as little under the dominion of vanity as possible, can behold the reflection of such a person in her glass, without pleasing sensations."

"Do you experience such?"

"I!—no, but we are wandering from the subject,—what was I saying? O, I remember, could Darnley behold you, thus lovely as you are, without becoming your slave? Were I a man, I know I should have been distractedly in love with you, and I make no doubt, should have given some extravagant proof of it. My brother admires pretty women, and yet I never heard him break out, as I should, in rapturous expressions of your beauty. He has a thousand times commended your internal perfections, yet those alone seldom make much impression on the heart of man."

"And yet," said I, "we frequently see women attracted by the mental qualities of a man, when his figure is far from engaging; and is not this a proof, my dear ladies, that our sex in general are not so very trifling and insignificant as the lordly men please to stile us? The outside figure of a man

man in my eyes is but the secondary cause of admiration, who admires the casket, when they know the value of the gem within? I declare, handsome as Lord Wilton is, I never thought of his person; had he been ever so unpleasing in his form, he must have had admirers in women of the least discernment."

"Lord Wilton is very amiable," said Louisa, with a sigh half suppressed, and a faint blush on her cheek, unperceived by any one but me.

Just then, a servant gave us notice Lady Darnley waited, we attended her, and were immediately summoned to the carriage. Sir George handed us in. He sat opposite to me. I observed he looked several times earnestly at me, with a scrutinizing eye, which gave me no pleasing sensation, as Harriot says, because he had "other thoughts" you know.

I had taken the resolution of appearing amazingly chearful, and chatted away with the rest of the ladies, ladies I repeat, for Sir George said very little.

When we arrived at the assembly, on entering the room, Lady Darnley escorted by her son, a gentleman, whose carriage preceded ours, offered his hand to lead me to a seat. The minuets had been begun some time. Soon after our being seated, the master of the ceremonies came up to me, and paid the usual compliment. When we were at the top of the room, he asked me, if there was any gentleman in particular, with whom I should chuse to dance. I could have answer'd him, without seeking far, but I chose to suppress my inclination. I said, all the gentlemen were equally strangers to me, but if that one, who stood next the music, had no dislike to dancing, I should have no objection to him. It was the
gentleman

MISS MELMOTH

gentleman who handed me in He readily embraced the opportunity of shewing his figure, I suppose, and likewise of dancing with me, to be sure

Won't you think me horrid vain, if I tell you all eyes were fixed upon your Caroline? But I am a coquet you know now I can amble a minuet tolerably at all times, but then excelled myself. No mercy upon my partner, nor the rest of the beaux But I must say something of the swain he took infinite pains to make his person, by no means bad, appear engaging to me, by throwing it in a thousand attractive attitudes, and to give me a proof of his wit and parts, he poured out a volley of soft things, to enumerate them, would fill a folio at least, but don't be uneasy, Sidney, I won't keep them all to myself

The minuet being over, my happy partner led me to my seat, through a throng of beaux, who bowed their thanks to me for gracing their assembly ——There's encouragement!

"Inimitable," said Harriot, "why, my dear, you have outdone your usual outdoings never did I see such a minuet before"

"Go, and excel me," said I

"Deuce take me, if I try," she replied "No, no, Sir," continued she to the master of the ceremonies, "I know when I am well off; I have no inclination to expose myself the rest of the ladies, I believe, had better follow my example."

Indeed most of them did, not above three minutes being danced after mine

"I think," said my partner, "we cannot tax the majority of these ladies with vanity, they are conscious of their inability to engage any one's attention after you"

"I don't

"I don't take that to be the cafe," faid I, "moft people think the time loft which is not devoted to country-dancing. I wifh I had not prolonged the time."

"I could almoft join in that wifh," faid he, fighing, "fince I muft lay my account to fuffer very much for the fight of fuch charms."

"O you will be no great fufferer I dare fay."

"I wifh it may not prove fo. But may I beg to know,—what I am afraid to be told,—are you engaged for the evening?"

"Then to eafe your pain a little, I am not."

"May I then hope to have the honor of your hand?"

"It is indifferent with whom I dance if you will accept an idle partner"—"Will accept!" his eyes fparkling, "I would fuffer all the torments the moft cruel tyrant could inflict, to have the honor, the blifs of preffing this lovely hand. Ah!" continued he, foftening his voice, "what joy beyond a mortal's fenfations muft the happy man experience who calls you his. Happy, thrice happy man! But is he here? will he not grudge me thefe few bleft moments?" "Who?" afked I, with furprize "who here?" "Your hufband" "My hufband!" repeated I, whom do you take me for? I have no hufband, I am not married!"

"Bleft founds! no hufband! I heard there was to be a bride here, who was the lovelieft of her fex wonder not then my eyes immediately fixed on you, as the perfon, where could they behold one equal to you?"

I hope I have repeated enough of this difcourfe, a difcourfe which you know me too well to think I could be pleafed with. No, my attention was otherwife engaged. Like a magnet Sir George drew me towards him, my eyes involuntarily followed

loved him. Ah! how infipid is every other man to him!

I foon joined in the dance, to prevent Mr Davenport, my new fwain, having an opportunity of talking more nonfenfe, he feeming to have a natural propenfity to it, as well as to be near Darnley, who danced with a Mifs Featherftone, a Bath acquaintance of his. he ufed to talk much of her. She, perhaps, is to be the happy girl. and yet he did not feem very affiduous neither, but he has lately been finding out many accomplifhments in her, which I own I cannot fee, tho' I endeavoured to diveft myfelf of prejudice as much as poffible.

Well, thank God, the affembly ended at laft. heartily tired I was, both of the dancing and my partner.

Lady Danley, and Louifa, who did not dance, went home long before us, fo there was only Sir George, Harriot, and myfelf. Harriot talked to me of my partner, of whom fhe faid, "I had made a conqueft, fhe was certain," and congratulated me upon it, faying, he was very rich, and half the miffes in the county were ready to pull caps for him, but it had no effect, for Mr Davenport was very difficult. but," continued fhe, " he has it now, I am fure,——I'll warrant it will do."

" It is not fo deep as a well, nor fo wide as a church-door, is it Harriot?"

" No, no, but he has it. Now don't you think him very handfome, Caroline? the cafket is not much amifs."

" No," faid I carelefsly, " not fo very handfome, but the man is well enough. tho' what think you, Sir George?"

" I think

"I think, Madam," rather peevishly, if Mr Davenport makes you the offer, you had better accept him."

"I thank you for your advice, tho' I did not ask it, Sir George, and if Mr Davenport should make me the offer, will certainly pay you the compliment of following it."

"He seems quite calculated for the meridian of your taste."

I was too much vexed to make any reply, surely, thought I, tho' he has " other thoughts," Sir George Darnley need not be rude.

Very little more conversation passed after this I was obliged to answer Harriot now-and-then, but Sir George opened not his lips, 'till we got home I took my leave immediately of Harriot Sir George withdrew the moment he handed us out of the coach, my young friend betook herself to rest, and I to my pen, as I before acquainted you, to scribble this uninteresting stuff to you I am really too tired to make any comments on the transactions of the preceding day You have a wretched, unentertaining friend, in

Your

CAROLINE MELMOTH

LETTER XXXIII

To Miss VERY

Darnley-Grove, June 27.

THIS morning Sir George rode out very early, as I was informed we had not his company at breakfast Soon after which, a servant announced Mr Davenport, he has, it seems, a

slight

slight acquaintance with the Darnley family. I could very easily have dispensed with the formality of his enquiring if I had taken any cold, &c He was in an elegant undress

I thought the man would never go;—I wanted to retire to my closet, to converse freely with my Sidney, to give ease to my troubled heart, but I could not with any propriety, as this visit seemed evidently on my account He was under a visible restraint,——I don't know how,——but, as if he thought his visit was already too long, and yet knew not how to take leave, I thought several times, he looked as if he would be glad of an opportunity, but could not avail himself of one, when it presented itself

His eyes did not please me,—being continually fixed on my face, than which I know nothing more disagreeable nay, it is to the last degree rude and ill-bred, what pleasure can the men find in staring a modest young woman out of countenance? Ah! how unlike——but the soft, timid glances I once fondly, fatally thought, were the indications of a secret flame, never had meaning or existence, but in my too, too credulous, self-flattering bosom——But this is a subject I must not trust myself with Ah, how ready am I, my dear Sidney, to fall into the theme!——Yet you see I check my too rash pen continually, but my heart, like the needle, is ever turning towards the pole, " and turning, trembles too."

Where was I? O, this Davenport After a long pause, which frequently happened, he resumed the subject of dancing again,---it had been worn almost threadbare before: Then said, " he had been down at Broom-Hill a very little time, otherwise," bowing circularly,--" he should have earlier solicited the honor of being countenanced by the good family, but hoped he might be allowed to flatter himſelf"——he ſeemed to be at no loſs in that point---" we would not refuſe his humble requeſt, when he begged to have our company at Broom-Hill, where he propoſed giving a little hop, which it would be his ſupreme happineſs to render as agreeable as was in his limited power."

What a ſtudied ſpeech was here! It came from the man, as if he had not been uſed to polite company——Not eaſy, natural, flowing, harmonious. He then, for the twentieth time, I believe, paid me a particular compliment on my laſt night's performance, much in the ſame eaſy way as the above recited ſpeech.

He reiterated his humble requeſt, as he called it. Lady Darnley anſwered for us girls, and did not doubt, ſhe ſaid, " but Sir George would think himſelf very happy in cultivating ſo agreeable an acquaintance."

He bowed, and ſimpered mightily, as much as to ſay, your Ladyſhip has a perfect eſtimation of my worth·——and ſo I believe ſhe has, for when he was gone, ſhe pronounced him a moſt finiſhed coxcomb. He appointed Friday to be the happy day, when, I make no doubt, he will think himſelf the happieſt man in the world, and feel the moſt ſatisfied. Happy ignorance! Did he ſee himſelf with my eyes—but he does not. He is bleſt with inſenſibility. How enviable would be the ſituation of ſuch people, were they capable of taſting real delight!

I muſt leave off ſcribbling.—Here Harriot comes to make an humble requeſt, ſhe ſays, which is, that I will honor her with my company in a walk in the Park.—ſhe will take no denial,—ſhe will come in and ſee what I am writing,—That would not be quite ſo proper, my friend Harriot——

Coming,

'Coming, coming, my dear hurrying girl—I shall not close my letter 'till my return. Adieu, for the present

Half past two.

The walk over, and dressing for dinner dispatched, behold me again in my closet

We rambled together in the park, Harriot rallying me on my imaginary conquest. She says she is certain this dance is meant as a compliment to me, and that he will be my partner—I hope not

When we had been walking a good while, I spied at a distance,—ah, how keen are the eyes of love!——Sir George sauntering in a melancholy posture. Surprised at the unexpected sight of him, I started, happily my companion did not perceive my emotion—Alas! what is the cause of his melancholy? I cannot, cannot bear to see him thus unhappy. But whatever is the reason, he appears so—Ah! would I could see him happy, were it in the arms of my greatest enemy! she could not long remain so, for I feel a natural propensity to love all he loves.——I must throw away this pen, Sidney! it is ever returning to the same subject——But is not the hand that guides, and the heart that dictates, equally culpable? acquit me if you can.

—But to proceed—Harriot did not see her brother, but accidentally led down the walk which led to that in which he was indulging, I fear, some unpleasing reflections However, we presently joined him He paid us the compliment of the morning—looked wretchedly!—my heart, without knowing the cause, sympathised with his countenance.

Harriot, the only one free and collected, kept up a spirited conversation almost by herself, and in her lively way, told Sir George of our engagement, and her surmises of the occasion—" You will go, Sir George?" asked I, thinking I must say something "I go!—what should I go for, no, madam, it will be sufficient if you ladies go"——" O pray, brother, go, I will take no excuse Miss Featherstone is to be there, and Captain Craven too! as poor Davenport thinks we are equally in love with our partners, as he is with his, therefore if you are so cruel as not to go, poor Miss Featherstone will be disappointed of her swain, besides, my mother has given her word you will be very happy"—" Happy!" interrupting her, " how should my mother know what will make me happy? and perhaps if she did, she might not be so ready, even if it was in her power, to render me so"

" Phoo! Sir George, what ails you? I was going to repeat her ladyship's speech to Mr Davenport,—Caroline's slave," " Dear Miss Harriot," said I, " how can you give the man such an appellation! I am sure there is no reason and if he was my slave, I should very soon free him from the severity of bondage"

[Observe, my dear Sidney, how easily one's words are misconstrued]

" You would not keep him long in bonds, I dare say,—you would soon exchange fetters with him "——These words, accompanied with a kind of sneer, and a half-averted face, would you think it? proceeded from the lips of Sir George Darnley What, Sidney, have I done, to deserve this treatment from him?——Would to heaven I was from hence! Any where in the world would be better, than to be hourly exposed to this cruel usage

Tears

Tears ſtarted into my eyes; but, thank God, unnoticed.

Harriot ſtill continued her intreaties to her brother, to induce him to accompany us to Broom-Hill—one while he would, then he would not, in ſhort, we left him quite irreſolute about it.

Unwilling to give him room to believe I was piqued at his cool, or rather contemptuous ſpeech, I affected to talk of Mr Davenport with pleaſure,——and among the reſt, aſked Harriot if ſhe did not admire his dreſſing, and choice of cloaths——You ſee by this how ill I played the diſſembler, to praiſe a man for the qualifications conferred on him by his taylor!

I know not to what it was owing, but Sir George was ſo petulant, neither his ſiſter nor I, [tho' I wonder not at myſelf, I have long ceaſed to pleaſe] could ſay a word which he did not find fault with.

Glad was I, when we reached the houſe. It was time to ſeparate for dreſſing, by which means I eſcaped the eyes of Miſs Darnley, who beholds me with more ſcrutiny than any one here. She is not happy,—dear girl! and perhaps perceives a ſympathy in me. Heaven forbid ſhe ſhould diſcover the ſecret workings of my rebel heart! She has great family-pride,——nor is any of them exempt from that pride, of which your poor Caroline can form no idea——How ſhould ſhe!——She who knows not from whom her birth is derived——But the laſt dinner-bell has rung. I muſt again leave top!——This is not poſt-day, ſo ſhall keep on ſcribbling, tho' I have nothing to ſay.

Eleven o'Clock.

A card in form this afternoon, from Mr Davenport, to enforce, as Harriot ſays, his eloquent embaſſy this morning.

Lady Darnley excused herself from going, I offered to stay to keep her company, and was very sincere, which you, my dear, will believe, tho' none present did, or at least would own

"I am greatly obliged to you, my dear Miss Melmoth; your offer is extremely polite, but I cannot think of depriving you of the pleasure and entertainment you will receive at Broom-Hill."

"I hope your ladyship will do me the honor to believe me when I affirm, I shall be much more satisfactorily entertained, if you will permit me to wait on you."

"Nay, nay, now you carry your obliging complaisance too far, my dear Caroline. I will not harbour so mean an opinion of your taste, to imagine you can really prefer the insipid conversation of an old woman, to the adoration of a sprightly young fellow. I am sure, at your age, I should not, tho' like you, I might have made the offer, and even appeared, thro' excess of good breeding, very well satisfied."

"If you think so ill of me, my dear madam, as to believe me insincere in my professions, punish me then by allowing me to stay with you."

"No, no," said she smiling, "the pretty things issuing from the lips of a pretty fellow, like Davenport,"---"Will give me no pleasure I if sure your ladyship."

"Don't fib, Caroline," said Harriot, "I am sure, what you said in the Park this morning, does not correspond with this affected coldness now."

The ladies immediately, without staying to hear my vindication, congratulated me, and called on Sir George to do the same.

"There is no occasion," said he coolly, rising "Miss Melmoth seems to have a high opinion of

Mr

Mr Davenport's merit; he therefore should be congratulated. She will, I make no doubt, be very happy with a man of his cast."

"Where are you going, Sir George?" said Lady Darnley; "you won't leave us?"

"I must beg your ladyship's excuse for a little while; I am rather remiss in not before paying my devoir to Miss Featherstone she is, I find, to be my partner next Friday, as Mr Davenport has judiciously paired us for that night, as he supposes we wish to be for life." He bowed, and quitting the room, said, "he must first make some little alteration in his dress, since that was the greatest charm with many ladies."---A hint for me, that

Oh! this Miss Featherstone! should he really love her, what will become of me? Good God, can it be possible! did he never love me? If he did, what have I done, to alter his sentiments? Why did I vainly hope?

The flatterer hope to my ruin led on,
And taught me to judge of his heart by my own,
Self-love, to my wish, was at hand to persuade,
That my love was return'd, and my friendship repaid.

But now,——

Its color false fancy no longer will lend,
To form the fond lover, or image the friend

Yet, was not his happiness my first, my sole wish? It was,——and is so still. If he can find it no where but with Miss Featherstone,——yes, Sidney, I will pray to heaven he may in her meet it ——May they be blest together, though your then poor broken-hearted Caroline will not long be witness of his felicity!

Vain, vain delusive hopes, whither, ah! whither are you fled?——too fondly cherished, where are the golden dreams you once excited?--Gone, for ever vanished.

Pardon me, my dearest Sidney, I have said a thousand times, I would not suffer my pen to resume this subject But my heart is refractory, it no longer listens to the dictates of reason,---passion hurries it with the impetuosity of madness.-- I must leave off -- I shall weary you to death with my fruitless inquietudes.

Ever your's,

CAROLINE MELMOTH

LETTER XXXIV.

To Miss VERE.

Darnley-Grove, July 1

THE important day is, thank heaven, over It would be tedious to relate the magnificence of the entertainment, or the self-applause glowing in the face of the entertainer, suffice it to say, art and nature were ransacked to render every thing superbly-inelegant, and politely troublesome,—at least so it appeared to me

The supper, profuse in every delicate viand,—dessert, consisting of hills and dales, purling streams and flowery vales,—and whatever beside you can think of

We were five-and-twenty couple —A curious group most of them —I am not in spirits,—or would endeavour to divert you with a description of some of the mules,---and their beauty, who, I

assure

assure you, came not far behind them, with their pigeon-winged hair——But the misses, my God! such fruz-towers! with every drawer and band box in their possession, emptied on their heads, you would have thought they had entered into an association, to keep each other in countenance---Yet they seemed all happy, self-satisfied---more than your Caroline could boast, I am sure Never did I pass a more disagreeable evening--compelled to listen to the nauseous flattery of that consummate fop Davenport.

I dressed myself in that painted sack which I began at your house last summer,---which you thought so pretty My swain shewed his immense taste and judgment, by paying me the most extravagant compliments

"Adorable Miss Melmoth, lovely in every dress!---from your appearance when I first saw you, I thought it impossible you could look so divine in any other———You have now, like the goddess of the spring, called forth the beauteous flowers, to make them blush, and hang their heads, envious it being so eminently outshone."---It was not in nature to answer this pompous flourish---I only bowed, and forced a smile, in which I infused a moderate share of the contempt I really felt for him ---The man, would you believe it,---thought I had given him encouragement, and ran on an age in the same delectable strain I hardly knew what he said,--my attention being sufficiently attracted by Sir George, and his fair partner, who were sitting tête a téte, he entertaining her, I make no doubt, from the animation of her features, with some agreeable topic.

Piqued with his assiduity, I pretended to receive the adulation of Mr Davenport with more complacency

We figured away in a minuet again---then began the country dances, and cotillons, performed much as ufual, and it being the fafhion to admire me,---met with the ufual applaufe.

After fupper, Davenport,---unwilling any of his talents fhould be wrapped up in a napkin,---hinted, that he was thought to dance the louvre tolerably, the provoking Harriot infifted on his performing it with me,---in vain I intreated to be excufed,--nothing would do---I muft obey the general voice ---I did not diftinguifh Darnley's, tho' "Full-fore againft my will, I exhibited" The man acquitted himfelf pretty well,---and if you will give him credit, I furpaffed the dancing of the angels ---I fancy he has little conception of angels.

I cannot dwell any longer upon a fubject, as pleafing as this---We broke up about four--When he---Davenport, I mean,--- intreated the permiffion to wait on me at the Grove

I faid, "I fuppofed Lady Darnley would be glad of the honor of his company"---He breathed out fome tender nonfenfe,---what, I did not heed,--nonfenfe I'm fure, it muft be.

We had a very dull ride home, which was eight miles; Sir George to the laft degree thoughtful and gloomy.

Louifa, who tenderly loves her brother, queftioned him on his late unufual gravity; he faid, he had been much troubled with a pain in his head ---he did not think himfelf well.

"It is well it is no more than head, Sir George," faid Harriot, "I was afraid there had been fome terrible commotion here"---tapping his breaft with her fan---" are you certain all is quiet and eafy here?"---" Mad girl!" faid he, " why all thefe interrogations!"

"Why

"Why I did not know but Mifs Featherftone might have made a buftle."---"Mifs Featherftone is a very amiable girl, I admire her exceedingly;---but"---he ftopped, and fighed The coach foon followed his example,---and we feparated

I am conftrained to write my letters piece-meal as the ladies are fo obliging they fay they cannot fpare me long---The time chiefly to myfelf is night, morning, and when we retire to drefs

Would to heaven I could write fomething more amufing to my amiable Sidney!---But if ever I had that faculty, it has forfaken me now It muft be an effort of politenefs,---or what is alone worthy praife, the innate goodnefs of your heart, if you find any charms in my correfpondence.

I know your tender fympathizing heart; and believe me, it is no fmall augmentation to my infelicity, that I am, as it were, compelled to make that heart a fharer in my pain---Yet that, alas! is my only confolation---Ought I to murmur at the decrees of Providence, bleft with fuch a friend as my Sidney? No. I will ceafe to complain of wayward fortune, left heaven fhould juftly punifh me, by depriving me of fo valuable a treafure,---and make me poor indeed.---I muft throw away my pen Adieu.

Saturday night, and Sunday morning

What a day have I fpent!---how been humbled!---Ah, my beloved friend why did you not check, in your Caroline, thofe feeds of pride which I have too long fuffered to flourifh in my heart?---but they have been plucked out by the roots, and are all blafted.---Yes, Sidney, I am now humbled to the duft, from whence having derived my haplefs origin, I have not the right of poffefling bleffings, in common with the reft of mankind.

I was

I was in my room this morning, and ruminating on the dull prospect before me, when I heard a carriage driving up the avenue, I looked up at the sound, and knew it to be Mr Davenport's I had no inclination to go down, and thought it would be time enough when I was sent for,---as I might suppose the visit was to Lady Darnley ---I own, I was rather surprised at hearing no message for near an hour,---not that I felt the least desire to see him, you may believe

In the midst of cogitations, fruitless to indulge, Frederic came up, with Lady Darnley's request I would favor them with my company.--I obeyed the summons, not with a very easy heart

Upon entering the room, Mr Davenport rose, and approached me with a bow, and a common place compliment,---two things he is always ready at,---took my hand, which I fain would have prevented, and led me to a chair next to Lady Darnley, seating himself next to me.---The form with which I was received, struck me amazingly

"My dear," said her ladyship, taking my hand, "I sent for you down, as I thought you did not know Mr Davenport was here."

I bowed

"I have requested the favor of his company to dine with us to-day, will you not"---looking at me with rather a significant smile---"join your intreaties, to prevail on Mr Davenport to oblige us?'"

Was not this a very singular address?

"Surely, madam, Mr Davenport can want no other inducement than the desire of your ladyship, unless he has some other engagement"

"No,----I have no other engagement I own, and if I could have vanity enough"---there seems no deficiency, thought I---" to hope my compliance
with

with the obliging requeſt of her ladyſhip, which does me the higheſt honor, would not be diſpleaſing to you"---ſighing

"To me, ſir!" with a ſurpriſe I could not conceal, "what right have I to be diſpleaſed with any gentleman of Lady Darnley's acquaintance viſiting her?"

"Then, madam, if it is not inconvenient, I will give myſelf the felicity of ſtaying "—bowing to each of us, which made it not particular

The young ladies ſoon after this came in, they had been to pay a viſit in the environs They did not ſeem at all ſurpriſed at ſeeing Mr Davenport, or hearing he was to dine with us,—which made me then think there was ſomething odd in it

Lady Darnley, amazingly ſtudious to entertain her gueſt, deſired Louiſa to give us a leſſon upon the harpſicord ſhe has, you know, a fine finger, ---ſhe performed vaſtly well Harriot then exhibited her talents, in one of Bach's overtures "My dear Miſs Melmoth, you will favor us?" ſaid Lady Darnley Davenport was on his feet in a moment, to hand me to the inſtrument —I played careleſsly, the firſt thing that came to hand,—but I excelled Orpheus all to nothing, you may be ſure I was then called upon by Mr Davenport, to add harmony to the ſounds by my angelic voice, which he was certain, by my natural melody in common ſpeaking, muſt be raviſhing when I exerted my vocal powers.—Cruel in me, you will ſay, to endeavour ſuch miſchief, but, contrary to the expectation of every one preſent, he ſurvived, to breathe out the moſt high-flown compliments that ever proceeded from the lips of one of the lords of the creation.

Sir George came home to dinner. He joined very little in the converſation,—nor indeed had he

opportunity,

opportunity, for Davenport, who abounds in small talk, exerted his loquacious faculty to the utmost. His behaviour was during the whole time so infuferably particular to me, I scarce knew how to act I chose rather not to underſtand him ſeveral times, as I was not enough at eaſe to anſwer his pompous ſpeeches in a ſuitable manner

After dinner, Sir George made an excuſe for not drinking tea with us, ſaying, "He was unfortunately engaged, before he knew we were to have the pleaſure of Mr Davenport's company, and was at the ſame time happy we were not in danger of miſſing him, ſince Mr Davenport would ſo abundantly compenſate for his abſence "

"Oh! my dear Sir George, you do me immenſe honor, upon my ſoul," ſhrugging up his ſhoulders, and bowing to the floor

About eight he took leave of us —Miſs Darnley told her ſiſter ſhe wanted to ſpeak to her, and drew her out of the room

Thus left alone with Lady Darnley, ſhe aſked me abruptly, how I liked Mr Davenport?——

"Like him, Madam?"

"Aye, my dear, don't you think him an agreeable man?"

"Upon my honor, Madam, to own the truth, I do not "

"No? why what objection can you have to him?"

"Objection, Madam?" ſmiling

"Why yes, my dear Caroline, I repeat, what objection can you have to Mr Davenport? unleſs, like too many young ladies, you find fault with a man for no other failing than beholding perfections in you "

"You amaze me, dear Madam, by this ſpeech, delivered too with ſuch ſeriouſneſs."

"Mr

"Mr. Davenport is serious, Miss Melmoth, in the most ardent passion for you."

"I am sorry for it."

"Sorry, my love! I am sorry to hear you say so. I did not indeed suppose you would betray a great satisfaction at first mention of it"——Betray, Sidney! so then it was not impossible I might feel a satisfaction—"But at the same time, I hoped, from the opinion I have ever had of your sense and prudence, and the knowledge I think I have of your heart"——I blushed, from the shame of having deceived her ladyship, in that heart——"I hoped, I say, you would have received the assurances of the distinction paid you by such a man, in a different manner."

"Ah! my dear Lady Darnley, you are displeased with me,"—and the tears started into my eyes,—"but I must hope your ladyship gave Mr. Davenport no encouragement."

"I will tell you all.—But why these tears, my dearest girl?—In me, behold your friend.—Mr. Davenport, after setting forth the fervency of his attachment to you, and making the most advantageous offers, begged I would inform him if your heart was disengaged; he did not doubt he had many rivals,——but if there was no favoured one, he would not give up his hopes. I took upon me to say, I was able to assure him, there was none; and I believed your heart was intirely disengaged."

"The heart must be disengaged indeed," with too much contempt, both in my looks and manner, ——"to find a place in it for Mr. Davenport." ——I perceived my error, by Lady Darnley's countenance, and would have rectified it, if possible; but she prevented me.

"Upon my word, Miss Melmoth, you must have a very high opinion of your charms, if you suppose

suppose, such men are to offer, and be refused every day by you. I don't mean to shock you, my dear, but you must be sensible, there are very few families, lovely as your person is, would overlook the deficiency you labor under."

"I am conscious of laboring under many deficiencies, Madam," my eyes fixed on the floor.

"Not one in your person or mind, my dear the deficiency I mean, is the ignorance of your origin. Every one can, no doubt, see your merit, but in alliances of this nature, people must pay some regard to birth ——your's is very mysterious, perhaps owing to a crime. I mean not to reflect on you, my sweet girl, children are not supposed answerable for the guilt of their parents —But circumstanced as you are, I think you ought to accept Mr Davenport's proposals. Consider, you are left intirely dependent upon the bounty of Mrs Gratton,—consequently your future prospects precarious. consider this, my love, on one side,——then change the scene, behold yourself mistress of Mr Davenport's house,—sharer in his heart and fortune ——what think you, Caroline, of this last point of view?"

"Oh! Madam, said I, weeping, "I see nothing but the despicable light in which I am unhappily placed. What?——should I repay this man for the honor he would confer on me, by giving him the hand of a beggar,—a base-born —No, Madam. I had indeed too great an opinion of myself, but your ladyship has kindly precipitated me from the hill of vanity, to the lowest vale of humility.—No, Madam, you have convinced me, I am not worthy even of Mr Davenport. Ah! my God!" continued I, rising with a fresh gush of tears, and lifting up my hands, " Ah! my God! why was I not born with a
sordid

…ordid heart, suited to my humble station?—why was it formed with aspiring wishes? why not low, mean and base, as my origin?

I know not what I said. The depreciating light I was set in, brought every presumptuous hope in judgment against me. I stopt myself, or I might in my agony of mind have betrayed the dearest secrets of my soul. I threw myself again in my chair, and covered my face with my handkerchief. Lady Darnley condescended to take the hand of this low creature, and pressing it to her lips, said, "My dear, my beloved Caroline, I intreat you to forgive me.—Indeed, indeed," and the tears trembled in her eyes,—"I did not mean to offend"—

"Offend me, Madam," rising and curtsying, with the utmost humility, "I can have no right to be offended with you, I may be wounded,—cut to the soul,———but must not, have not a right to complain."

"Nay, now, my dear Caroline, I am sure you are angry with me"——And she tenderly threw her arms round my neck, and kissed my burning cheek. But come, compose yourself. I was much to blame, I own. I felt myself rather displeased at your manner of refusing so advantageous an opportunity of advancing yourself in life—— an opportunity so seldom to be met with, especially when I had given Mr Davenport some reason to believe you would not be so cruel. But you must promise me, my dearest Caroline, that you will see him the day after to-morrow, or I shall think you have not yet forgiven me."

"Ah! my dear Madam, do not make such a request; I cannot bear to see any one. Permit me to retire.—I must learn a new lesson: I have a proud—

proud———I find I have, and stubborn heart;———I must teach it to bend,———or break it in the attempt."

"I cannot bear my own reflections,———they are too humiliating,—too degrading. I wish I could retire from the knowledge of all the world.—I never arrogated much merit to myself, yet still infinitely more than I ought.———Every one too by their praises, and countenancing the hapless orphan, contributed to inspire ambition in me, but the flame is now intirely extinguished, I now see every thing in its proper light.———Permit me, Madam, to leave your presence. it is necessary to implore the divine assistance, to attain the knowledge of myself."

"Amiable girl! how does my affection increase for you each moment!———What delicacy, what nobleness of sentiment!———But do, my dearest Caroline, promise me you will see and converse with Mr Davenport on Monday,———only oblige me."

"I will endeavour to obey your ladyship,—but I cannot consent to give him any encouragement. I dare not call it innate, but sure I have acquired it from the polite and truly worthy people I have lived among; but I find so great a compunction in the thoughts of being guilty of bestowing my hand without my heart, that your ladyship must excuse me. Mr Davenport has not,———nor is it in his power to make any impression on that heart,—which, low as the possessor is, has yet never harboured an ill thought."

"Well, my dear, I do not doubt your prudence will suggest a proper mode of behaviour."

"As an acquaintance of your ladyship's, and in deference to your better judgment, I will behave

have towards him with politeness and strict justice."

I was then permitted to withdraw. I hurried up to my room, and threw myself on my knees, with an intent to pray for an humble mind, and strength to bear my distresses, but I was too disturbed,——my tears and sobs deprived me of all power of reflection. I leaned over the side of the bed a considerable Time. I then rose, and traversed the room without any meaning; I threw myself into a chair, where I remained motionless, with my eyes fixed on the carpet, 'till a servant informed me supper was ready. Being quite unfit to appear, I sent excuses to the ladies, which were accepted. When I had recovered a little, I sat down, to give you a detail of my unhappy train of affairs. I dare not trust myself to make any animadversions, I should run to too great lengths.

Ah! my dear, my beloved Sidney! can you, will you still continue your friendship to the poor degraded, and truly distressed

CAROLINE MELMOTH.

LETTER XXXV.

To Miss VERE.

Darnley-Grove, July 4.

MY conference with Mr Davenport gave me inexpressible pain in apprehension. I saw, at least fancied I saw, very little of true delicacy in him. what could I therefore do with such a man? Unlike Sir John Evelin in every respect. I perceived a consciousness in his manner, which

which seemed to say, while he was professing himself my slave, he would, when I was in his power, convince me of the contrary. In short, he is the man, of all I have seen, least likely to make any impression on my heart.

In compliance with Lady Darnley's request, I consented to see him. I was left (one by one dropping out of the room) alone with him——He, with great parade, endeavoured to make me sensible of the honor he designed me; for such, I dare say, he thought he was conferring. I heard him to the end, and then begged he would likewise attend to what I had to say. I intreated him to believe, I was abundantly convinced of the honor he did me; but at the same time, should be wholly unworthy his distinction, were I not to treat him with sincerity, which, however unpleasing it might be to him, I certainly could not acquit myself of injustice unless I did.

I then proceeded to point out to him, how absolutely necessary to constitute happiness in the marriage state, it was, that there should be a parity of sentiment, which, I must say, I could not perceive between us——

Mr Davenport interrupted me, saying, "If there is not a parity of sentiment, my dear Miss Melmoth, it convinces me, I have been, and still am in an error, from whence I never can emerge, but by your bright example. Permit me then to hope, most divine, adorable creature, that my love and unremitted assiduity may one day induce you to pronounce a more favorable doom."

"I should despise myself, Sir, were I a moment to keep you in suspence, when I am certain, my decision can never be in your favor. Let me then beg of you, to lay aside the thoughts of pro-

secuting your suit any further; it will be in vain
I ask your pardon, Sir, but on such an occasion,
to be evasive, would be unjust."

" Ah, Madam," throwing himself at my feet,
" do not; oh! do not at the same time pierce my
heart with your cruelty and goodness. I cannot,
ah! do not urge it, I cannot yet relinquish my
hopes. Lady Darnley assured me your heart was
disengaged. I have no favored rival.—the rest I
value not. Whoever makes pretensions to you,
must wade thro' every drop of my blood."

He really startled me, by his air and tone.
" Rise, Sir, rise, you terrify me,—I beg you
will rise."

" Never, never, by Heavens, unless you give
me some shadow of hope."—

" Would you then be contented with the shadow,—or will you constrain me to leave the
room?"

" Ah! replied he, sighing, and rising, cruel as
you are, you must be obeyed. But tell me, lovely,
beauteous creature, have I not (notwithstanding
Lady Darnley assured me to the contrary) a rival?
Too sure, I must. perhaps, ye Gods, a favored
one———Say, oh! say, who is the destined
wretch?"

" When you can convince me, Sir, you have
any authority to interrogate me thus, I may be in-
duced to answer your question.—You ought to be
satisfied with my ingenuous sincerity. and, with
all deference to your merit, Sir, I think it possible
for a woman to refuse even Mr Davenport, without having her heart under the influence of any
other engagement."

"Ah, Madam, I am but too sensible of my
want of merit, to engage the affections of so amiable a lady. yet I hoped, my earnest endeavours to
please

please, might in time have conquered your indifference. nor should I think---were it my whole life --the time ill-spent, could I flatter myself at last I was not disagreeable to you"

"I assure you, Mr Davenport, when the man I can like, addresses me, he will not need to spend his whole life in inducing me to indulge the dictates of my heart I will deal with the same open sincerity towards him, I have used to you —And now, if you please, we will seek the ladies"—Saying which, I led to the door, and bowed to him to follow he did not, but continued in a fixed posture

When I entered the room where the ladies were, they looked at me with enquiring eyes —Harriot first broke silence

"Well, how have you disposed of your swain? —how have you behaved to him?"

"Acted, as I promised her ladyship I would, obeyed the dictates of prudence and justice"

"And how was that, my good girl?"

"Acquainted Mr Davenport, Madam, how very dishonorable it would be to accept his hand, while my heart could not even feel the gratitude it owed for his noble offer."

At this instant, a servant entered, with Mr Davenport's compliments, and begged to have an audience of Lady Darnley

Both Miss Darnleys wondered I could refuse such an offer; but commended me very much for my sincerity, and wished I might meet with a man suitable to my worth, and so forth —

Lady Darnley soon returned, and told me, she could not prevail on Mr Davenport to give up his hopes time, he said, might produce something in his favor, with the interposition of friends —He
could

ould not absolutely despair, while I was single, or
he had no rival.

I said, I could not help it.—I had nothing to accuse myself of, but stood acquitted to my own heart, in regard to my behaviour to him ---And hoped, he would be no further troublesome to the family, or me, by his fruitless importunity.

I have not yet recovered my late conference with Lady Darnley it hangs heavy on my heart Ah! was that stroke wanted to depress me still more?

I have not seen Sir George since yesterday morning He went not to church with us, but rode out, he returned late at night, after we had separated, this morning he went out a hunting---I hope he is happier than your friend

July 5

Ah! Sidney, I may now indeed set about the task I ought to have finished long ago,---the subduing my heart. I am now convinced

I wandered down one of the avenues of the garden this afternoon, when, seated in a little alcove at some distance, I beheld the most amiable of men ---yet, yet I must call him so,---a book lay by him He was in a melancholy posture, leaning his head upon one hand, the other held a miniature, on which his eyes were fixed intently; I thought I saw his bosom heave with sighs He pressed the picture to his lips and breast,---but still retained his attitude and pensive air I had seen enough Ah! my dear Sidney, he loves, it is plain Alas! is it not equally evident he is not happy?---He, like your poor Caroline, loves,---but loves in vain. I know not how I got in doors, or up to my chamber I found myself there more dead than alive.

Heavens! is it possible such a man can be rejected---forsaken? Whoever it is, she must have given him

him her picture Who can it be? Not Miss Featherstone!---This is no new impression.

I tire myself, and rack my brains, but cannot draw any conclusions from my study---Time may unravel the mystery.

Adieu, my dearest Sidney. pray for the recovery of all our peace.

CAROLINE MTIMOTH

LETTER XXXVI.

To Miss VERE.

Darnley-Grove, July 8

AH! what shall I do? He is ill---He is in distress---The dear, the amiable Darnley is indisposed---Ah! how altered he is!---he sighs---looks pale---pensive, yet tells not his pain---My God! who should he tell it to?---He loves, I am convinced Ah! who can be cruel to him!---and yet it must be so O! too well I know the symptoms He eats not I heard him too last night traversing his room, he cannot rest---Ah! who is it that occasions his grief? O that I knew! Had I influence over the lovely maid, I should not long behold him wretched Did she but know his worth, as I do---his noble, generous nature it would be impossible for her to resist him Had she but seen him, as I have, soothing distress, and chearfully assisting the weak, the tear of humanity glistening in his lovely eyes, when he could only give pecuniary comfort! O Sidney! is it in nature to give pain to such a heart?

July 9

Do not, ah! do not, my charming friend, condemn my sensibility, a sensibility which can only cease

cease with my existence. I am sure my tenderness for him is closely connected and interwoven with my whole system.—I weep, Sidney, but it is for him I weep was not my whole soul filled with his image, I should weep for the distress of such a man

* * *

My God! a letter from Mrs Grafton Why this trembling—this perturbation,—what should it mean?—I have not power to break the seal—yet why?—Ah, Heavens! there is one enclosed from Davenport.—Grant me your pity, Sidney, I must, if my swoln eyes will permit me, peruse this much dreaded epistle from the best of women

* * *

My fears were greater than the danger Dear, amiable Mrs Grafton! She leaves me at liberty, after urging her ardent wishes to see me happily settled, to reject Mr Davenport, if I cannot give him my heart.—Alas! my kind benefactress, I have none to bestow She then repeats a conversation she had with that gentleman, she avoids giving her opinion of him, as she would lay no restraint upon my actions, which, she tenderly says, shall ever be free.—She wishes I could make an election mentions an overture made to her some time since, for her interest with me in favor of Mr Blagrave, but is certain, a man of his stamp will never make me the happy wife she wishes to see me

Mr Davenport assured her, Lady Darnley was his advocate She need not remind me of the great affection shewn me by herself and family. and concludes, by telling me, she will with pleasure ratify and countenance any choice I shall make, as she is certain such choice will never be an improper one and further adds, from the apparent

Vol I   H   sincerity

sincerity of Mr Davenport's passion, he shall make it her constant prayer, the man I may hereafter choose, may have the same

Dear, amiable Mrs Grafton! shall I have your prayers? The prayers of such a worthy soul must be efficacious if you are my intercessor at the throne of grace, I will not despair of yet being happy

She is firmly persuaded I shall make a proper choice! Ah! Sidney, are not our conceptions of impropriety widely different?—But perhaps she does not see me in so very low a light as Lady Darnley—or the rage of family-pride has not such power in her kind, compassionate bosom

I shall say very little of Davenport's letter It is filled with fine compliments, and ardent professions of a passion he must still indulge—hopes, which he can never relinquish while I continue single Nor will he—for which he intreats my pardon on his knees—yield up his pretensions to any man living Insolent creature! He did not shew his letter to Mrs Grafton surely—she would not in the least have been his advocate I am certain

In rather a commanding way for so abject a slave as he sometimes appears to be, he begs to be heard once more He says, he shall come to Lady Darnley's, there if I do not condescend to grant him five minutes audience, he shall be the most unhappy wretch breathing Still insists, there must be some favored lover, altho' Mrs Grafton, as well as Lady Darnley, have assured him to the contrary—But his final doom must be pronounced by my own lips

I wish the man would take his answer—I will not see him, if I can avoid it without giving offence to Lady Darnley—But yet, after all, it my dear
Mr

Mrs Grafton, who is in the place of the tenderest of mothers, leaves me at liberty to reject him, or any one I cannot approve, why should I so much dread Lady Darnley's displeasure? unless it is, because she is the parent of Sir George---aye, there's the point

I ventured to inquire of Frederick just now, of Sir George Darnley's illness.---He is an excellent servant, and loves his master.---Ah! who lives that does not!

He acquainted me, Sir George had not slept, and appeared very much disordered---fancied something lay upon his mind, which disturbed him I dared not trust myself to hold further converse with him, but hurried to my room to conceal my tears, which were fast gathering to my eyes ---They hardly ever cease to flow when I am alone, and it is with no small difficulty I restrain them when in company.

Lady Darnley, who doats on her son, is very unhappy at his indisposition; herself and the young ladies, are continually with him How ardently do I long to join my tender care to theirs! is not my anxiety greater than theirs can be? Yet tyrant custom renders my attendance on him an absolute impropriety They assure me, he is not in danger ---Ah! the least surmise of such a thing throws me into an agony

I steal out sometimes unperceived, and place myself close to his door—listen attentively to every found, then, for fear of a discovery, hurry back to my room, sit down—rise up—walk about—uneasy—restless—tire every chair—weep---dry my eyes --resolve to appear composed---and burst into a fresh flood of tears, augmented by the means used to stop them.

I have more time to myself now——'twas what I wished, but ah! my God! 'tis the illness of the most amiable of men which occasions it.—I am fretful——every body displeases me——but most of all, Davenport, who pesters me with letters I have opened two or three, but seeing his name at the bottom, have torn them to pieces.——I will return them for the future unopened——He is wretched——he is undone, unless I will deign to receive him, for what,——my God!——my husband!——Let him be wretched——I cannot help it——I am sure I sought not to make him so ——he cannot be so wretched as I am, he has not enough of sensibility

Sir George's illness has prevented his coming here at present, but he does not yet despair.—Vain, impertinent man!

Were he possessed of the least degree of delicacy, I would frankly own my partiality for another, but he would immediately disclose it to Mrs Grafton, and the rest of my friends——and then I should be deprived of my only happiness——But what after all is that, but the repeated opportunity of deceiving myself into misery, and tiring you with the dull repetition of my folly?

* * *

July 12

I write but a few lines at a time I am not sufficiently myself to do more, so that this letter has been the employment of several days Sir George is enough recovered [Heaven be praised!] to come into the dressing-room.—Ah! how I wish, yet dread to see him! His sisters say, he is much altered —Ah! how will he appear in the eye of love? I must summon all my fortitude to my aid, lest I betray myself.—Support me, Heaven, the hour is come.—What a tremor! It possesses my whole
frame

frame Harriot is coming to me—I muſt go down, ſhe ſays, there is a perſon impatient to ſee me—What can ſhe mean?——ſhe looks with pleaſure ſparkling in her eyes—yet tells me not who is impatient to ſee me—My trembling limbs will ſcarce ſupport me—yet go I muſt. Adieu

CAROLINE MELMOTH.

To Miſs VERE, in continuation.

Cruel Harriot! yet her cruelty proceeds from her ignorance of the ſtate of my heart, and what I ſuffer-- Ah! did ſhe know what anxious doubts ---doubts! no, the racking certainties I hourly endure---ſhe would not,---ſhe ſurely would not thus, by trifling, add to a diſtreſs already too ſevere.

I followed her tottering into the dreſſing-room. The firſt object that met my view, was the dear Darnley on a couch, pale---languid---I approached him, not without emotion, to pay my congratulatory compliments on the recovery of his health, he received them with his uſual grace, but trembled thro' exceſſive weakneſs---I felt myſelf all in a tremor, from a thouſand different motives. He made an ineffectual effort to riſe. I ſtood by him, and was going to ſay ſomething to him, when ſomebody attempted to take my hand. "Have you then no compaſſion left for me?---me, whom you by your cruelty have reduced to a ſtill worſe ſtate than is Sir George by illneſs!"

I turned haſtily round at the beginning of this ſpeech---It was Davenport, who was impatient to ſee me---I had flattered myſelf, my dear Sidney, as uſual---ever induſtrious in tormenting myſelf---I coloured from vexation and diſappointment, and felt myſelf ſtrangely diſconcerted.---I knew not what to say, and foolishly remained silent. I condemned myself at the time, but infinitely more on recollection of my silly behaviour—yet really I had not then the power of utterance.—Indeed, all things duly considered, it may very easily be accounted for.—But now I must acquaint you with a circumstance, which I before forgot to relate.

One day Lady Darnley, during the confinement of Sir George, expressed her surprise at not seeing Mr Davenport.—"Why should your ladyship be surprised?" said I. "is the inconstancy of man very strange? Besides, I really think Mr Davenport has acted very properly, and quite to my satisfaction, in not continuing his visits, for was he to lay his account with my complying with his wishes, he would only, I am afraid, subject himself to a disappointment.—"You are really then resolved, my dear"—"With regard to Mr Davenport, madam, firmly."

"I wish you would let reason be your guide, Caroline, for a little while; it would induce you to think more favourably of Mr. Davenport's offer."

"I shall ever think Mr Davenport has done me honor. It is pain to me to be obliged, without the power to make a return, yet such has ever been my lot. But it would be the highest ingratitude in me, to endeavour to deceive him, and the only method I could think of I put in practice, to repay the obligation he conferred on me, namely, fairly and ingenuously assuring him, I never could think of him in the way he would have me. I have told him so—why cannot he be contented?" "No, my dear," returned Lady Darnley, "the man who has once formed hopes of possessing you, cannot be so easily contented, or he could not love you at all Perhaps you may not be, what the world calls in love, with Mr Davenport, but from your own knowledge of mankind, and the great good fense you are miftrefs of, you muft have remarked, that violent love-matches very feldom turn out happy; you have likewife fo high and juft a fenfe of the duties in focial life, that you would endeavour to act conformable to thofe duties, and your endeavours, I make no doubt, would be crowned with fuccefs"

" I dare not run the rifk," replied I, fighing, and fhaking my head

" You promifed me, to treat him with politenefs"

---" And juftice, remember, madam," fmiling

" Well, well, I know that But do you likewife remember, my dear Mifs Melmoth, though Mrs Grafton has kindly left the difpofal of your hand to yourfelf, fhe yet wifhes to fee you happily fettled, and where then has an opportunity offered like this?"

" Such a one, it is true, madam, may never offer again, nor do I wifh it, as I am certain I fhould act in the fame manner." I paufed---Did I not go too far? I thought I had, and checked myfelf immediately, adding,---" Provided I felt the fame indifference for the perfon, as I did for Mr Davenport---But my dear Lady Darnley, this is to me a very unpleafing topic, will you permit me to drop it?---How does Sir George? may I not congratulate you on his amendment?"

" Yes, thank God! my dear, Sir George is a great deal better in health, but his fpirits are ftill very weak. I cannot imagine the caufe of the depreffion he feems to labour under, I hope it is only owing to the remains of his fever"

H 4 " I hope

"I hope so too," said I, suppressing a sigh with great difficulty.

"I must go to my son---But will you promise me, should Mr Davenport come, you will remit a little of your cruelty towards him?---

"---Would you wish me to give him encouragement, when---" "No, no, my dear, be not so hasty, but you may treat him as one of my friends."

"I wish he requested no other from me, I would readily pay that respect due from me to every friend of Lady Darnley's."

"If you do not" said she, "after all I have thought to the contrary, I shall believe your affections are engaged, and then what am I to think." Thank heaven, Lady Darnley did not fix her eyes upon me at that instant, if she had, she must have discovered my secret by my confusion: I felt as if a million of needles and pins were stuck in my face and throat---"Well then, madam," I answered at last with some difficulty, "my behaviour, and not my words, shall convince you, but I will detain you no longer." I arose, she did the same---I accompanied her to the door of Sir George Darnley's room, and then retired to mine.

You will say, my silent fit lasted me a long time on the suddenness of Mr. Davenport's address, but I thought it necessary, my dear, to make you acquainted with the preceding incident, to account for the civility of my deportment towards him, which I used merely to take off the suspicion, which Lady Darnley seemed beginning to entertain but I am so bad a dissembler, that I was in great danger several times of over-acting the part I assumed.

But

But let me see where I was, when I began this long digreffion.---I fuffered Mr. Davenport to detain my hand fome time before I had power [all the above in my head] to withdraw it, as foon as I recovered my fpeech, I made fome trifling remonftrances to him, on his furprifing me in fuch a manner,---and fat down ---He took a chair next to me, and begged I would give him a hearing this he fpoke in a very low voice " " Whifpering, you know," faid I, " is not polite at any time, and now it is unneceffary, fince you may fay all you have to fay, aloud "

I then, to prevent his faying any thing difagreeable to me, talked of indifferent things to Mifs Darnley We foon entered on general topics, in which we all could join, except indeed Sir George, who hardly ever opened his lips

Dinner being foon ready, relieved me from the apprehenfion of Mr Davenport's particularity of behaviour to me and in the afternoon company came in, fo, upon the whole, I had not much to complain of. I behaved with a freedom [my fpirits being raifed by Sir George's recovery] and eafe, to which I have fome time been a ftranger. Davenport made an unmerciful long vifit, confidering it was to a fick man I was heartily glad, when he bethought himfelf that it was high time to depart Lady Darnley feemed very much to approve of my conduct her eyes frequently told me fo

Mifs Cathcart and her brother ftayed the evening We retired each to our feparate apartments, as foon as they left us, by which means I avoided any *eclairciffement* with Lady Darnley, of which I was not forry.

I can write no longer---It is very late: and I muft indulge my drowfy fit, which, ftealing upon me, me, invites me to flumber——Adieu, my beſt love

Your's,

CAROLINE MELMOTH

LETTER XXXVII

To Miſs VERE

Darnley-Grove, July 15

SIR George (thank Heaven) recovers his ſtrength daily, but not his ſpirits. He talks of going for a few days to Mr Stanhope's, a friend of his at ſome diſtance from hence, in hopes the change of air will be of ſome ſervice to him.—Heaven ſend it may prove propitious to his wiſhes! He removes from Darnley-Grove to-morrow. How dull——how dreary will the time appear in h abſence! And yet, circumſtanced as I am, ought I not ardently to wiſh it! Should I not rejoice, at an event, which will afford me an opportunity of beginning a work I ought long ere this have concluded——recovering my wonted ſerenity? But all the methods I could now uſe, would have no effect. I ſhould ſuffer too much pain from the experiment, beſides, I have not faith that I ſhould ſucceed, after the ſevereſt attempts. Things are now come to ſuch a paſs, they muſt e'en take their own courſe, and perhaps I may ſay with Richard, " For this, among the reſt, was I ordain'd."

We are to go an airing with Sir George the firſt time, this morning.—I thought ſince, I might have deſired to be excuſed, as five, though the coach is large, is rather above the complement,

eſpecially

especially as an invalid is of the party, but I simply considered, we (you see I include myself) are to lose him to-morrow.

I fancy the person who affirmed, that love seldom survived hope, knew very little of the passion at least he must allow the old saying, of no general rule without an exception; for am not I a woeful example, that such a thing is possible? For I would be glad to know, what hopes, reasonable ones I mean (and yet, who ever thinks of reason in love?) I could absolutely build on—none, no, not one every thing against me, and my own self-deceiving-heart on my side——" Hopes I could have none, for I was all despair" even from the first,——and yet I loved! I should not then complain of Mr Davenport, perhaps, since I am so culpable myself, yet I hope there is not a great similarity neither between us, I at least keep my unhappy passion to myself——except indeed, tormenting my dear Sidney with it but you were desirous of having my whole heart before you—and a fine employ it is for you, no doubt But if my example can preserve you from falling into the same snare, I shall not have suffered in vain. If I am not worthy to be made a pattern, use me as an example—they are, generally speaking, of most use to the world

The coach is coming to the door —Adieu, my beloved Sidney.—I am impatient to hear from you, suffer me not to remain long in that state

It is not worth while to send you this short letter, I will not therefore close it till evening · tho' I do not promise, I shall be able to fill my paper with any occurrence worthy your perusal But if you will correspond with me, it must be as a man takes a wife, for better for worse, and I am afraid, the comparison will hold good in
many

many inftances, particularly, that the bad too
often preponderates but if I had any thing pleaf
ing to communicate, you fhould have your fhare

In Continuation

Our jaunt in itfelf was pleafant enough, that is,
the fun fhone,—the birds fung,—and the hedges
yielded their fweeteft odours

But not in itfelf the gay profpect can pleafe,
We only can tafte when the heart is at eafe

Which not being altogether the cafe with you,
friend, you may fuppofe, " the air appeared nox
ious,—the birds too offended," not indeed, becaufe
my love was away, but from reafons to you abundantly obvious Lady Darnley too did not much
contribute to enliven the fcene within the coach
—at leaft to me, for fhe continually was talking of
Davenport for from my laft behaviour to that
gentleman, fhe encourages hopes that I fhall full
remit my cruelty, as fhe ftiles it, towards him
Quere now, whether it would not be more crual
to devote him for life, to a woman who almoft
hates him, and, perhaps, whom in a few months
he may feel more averfion for, than he even now
pretends love to?—He is not a favourite of Sir
George's, I believe he defpifes him Could I
marry a man defpifed by Sir George Darnley?

He faid, he was a man of indifferent morals,—
nor had he much pretenfion to fenfe [This was
during our airing] " But I beg your pardon, Mifs
Melmoth, I fhould be cautious what I fay of Mr
Davenport, before you."——" You have my
leave to fay what you pleafe of Mr Davenport,
Sir George I will promife not to be offended "

" You put me in mind, Caroline, of a lady I
have heard of, who not only was not offended
when

when she heard a gentleman vilified, but joined in it with the greatest acrimony, at the time she was secretly engaged to marry him the next day."

" Is the resemblance a striking one, Miss Harriot?" asked I, smiling. Sir George too smiled. " I have not vilified Mr. Davenport, Harriot."— " Nor have I joined in it" said I, " with acrimony. Mr Davenport may have many perfections, and as many vices to counter-balance them —but it is best for me to be silent on that head."

Till Lady Darnley commended me for my speech, it did not occur to me I had been guilty of any impropriety, but could I have said otherwise, if I had really intended to give Mr Davenport's address sanction.

When we returned, we found a card to Lady Darnley, intimating Mr Davenport's intention of doing himself the honor of taking a family-dinner with her to-morrow.—Deuce take the man, he is very fond of doing himself honor.—If he was desirous of doing me pleasure, he would take himself far enough another way.—We were to have attended Sir George part of the way to Wellborough, the seat of Mr Stanhope; but O, by no means now, as Mr Davenport is to give us his company.

Lady Darnley's wishes and intentions are worthy her noble heart—she is not acquainted with the secret workings of mine; and as marriages go now-a-days, to be sure, this is a very eligible one in the eye of the world. But Lady Darnley is a woman of much too good sense, to run current with the opinion of the world, true —But then, I have no family-considerations—or if I had, they would not avail,——since Mr Davenport's family is not one of yesterday————one that only prizes itself in coming over with the
Conqueror

Conqueror—for such, with Lady Darnley, are families of yesterday. On her own side, she can trace back a chain of ancestors, famously conspicuous long before that epoch; and the Darnley family have ever looked on those with contempt, who have lost their names, and tarnished their glory, by accepting titles.—O Caroline, Caroline, what a fool wert thou, ever to harbour a thought exceeding esteem for any part of such a family!—And yet, were that period of my life to be repeated, my folly would likewise take place, I dare say. For how could I guard against a danger I did not suspect? Ah! who that beholds his lovely face, and contemplates the virtues beaming there, will ever suspect mischief in so bright a form? The pleasing enemy was so gentle in his approaches,——its galling chains were hid by soft-bewitching smiles. Nor did I ever think of asking my heart the nature of the attachment I felt for Sir George, " 'till a sigh gave the omen, and proved it was love." Then, O, then it was too late to recede. No, the enemy had taken possession of the garrison, nor would allow any quarter, though the governor had been surprised into danger, which perhaps no human precaution could have prevented.

This affected raillery, my dear, is all grimace, under the semblance of a smile, your Caroline carries an aching heart.——Ah, when will it be at peace?

There are in grief, as well as joy, (while perhaps neither can be accounted for) seasons when we are not equally sensible; mine is not so poignant at present, as it has been, and yet my situation is virtually the same the same hopes (I blush to say) to delude,—the same misery to fear. But sometimes I argue thus, Why do I give way to sorrow,

sorrow, nay, oftentimes take it up at a large interest?——Will not pain come to us with swiftness enough without our solicitations?—Or will my excessive dejection of spirits retard or forward events, which will, let me act as I please, take place?

Don't think I am a predestinarian, by my last expression, I am far from being so, on the contrary, I believe our fate depends intirely on ourselves, as to actions. It is destroying the very essence of a benign Being to think otherwise. Can we suppose a merciful and just God would create us only as machines, to execute evil, which is pre-ordained, and then, after a life of misery, or at best dissatisfaction, the inseparable companions of time ill-spent, to punish us everlastingly in a world to come?—What an impious system! Destroying the most glorious attributes of a divinity! making him a creature, delighting in cruelty, and, like envy, exulting over prostrate wretchedness! And admitting it possible any one in their senses can really believe such doctrine, how dangerous to be inculcated! Where is the merit of virtue, or the iniquity of vice, if we destroy the opinion, rooted naturally in our minds, of free agency?

I only mean, I ought not to look into future events, for causes to grieve, for surely, to me "sufficient to the day, is the evil thereof." Were we to estimate our rewards by our deserts, we should not be so ready to complain perhaps, for who, humanly speaking, merits the innumerable blessings we daily——nay hourly enjoy, without acknowledgment or gratitude for them? or if we think of them at all, we too frequently attribute them to accident. A logician would tell us, there is no such thing as accident, tho' we continually cry such or such a circumstance happened accidentally

accidentally, without at all confidering, how many concurrent circumftances muft fall out to make this accident, which appears fo trifling— Before we even eat,——the fun muft have fhone —the rain muft have defcended—the hufbandman muft be in a difpofition to work—the wind muft blow—and fo on of a thoufand things which would afford fpeculation to an enquiring mind, did not the frequency of thefe contingencies render them habitual, and confequently difregarded

But you will fancy, my frenzy has taken a different turn, if I go on in this ftile, and that I am grown philofophically mad, but were you to fee me, you would difcover the fymptoms which denote the mad lover, in which character, I fear, I fhall live and die Let me be as I will, I fhall be ever

Your's

CAROLINE MELMOTH

LETTER XXXVIII.

To Miſs VERE

Darnley-Grove, July 16

SIR George has juft left us What could he mean? He alarmed me I have not yet recovered myfelf What weak mortals we are! the moft trifling incidents thus to affect one Lord! how I tremble! I again repeat, what could he mean? I have afked myfelf this fimple queftion a thoufand times, yet cannot anfwer it I cannot write I will endeavour to collect my fcattered thoughts,

thoughts, and, when a little composed, will inform you of the reason of this perturbation

*   *   *

We had but a dull breakfast, as you may imagine, every one chusing to keep their thoughts to themselves, though they may easily be guessed at. Lady Darnley and her daughters were anxious about the beloved son and brother I need not spend much time in defining the nature and source of my uneasiness Sir George too was melancholy I once ventured to raise my eyes to his face—I perceived his fixed on me with a softness I have not a long time beheld in them, I thought too——I might be mistaken——he sighed, when he removed them I felt I know-not-what of confusion, my heart seemed too big for my bosom I asked Lady Darnley (in order to conceal my emotions) some question about the tea, but in so hurrying a kind of way, that Harriot asked me, if I had burnt my lips with it —I know not what answer I returned

When this repast was dispatched, we separated Sir George was to go at eleven.

I went, hardly knowing what I did, into Miss Darnley's dressing room——I could not write—I had not been there long—my work in my hand, which by the bye I could not touch, I was so agitated when Sir George came in with Miss Darnley. They seated themselves Louisa talked of her brother's excursion,—hoped he would find benefit from it, &c I joined in the same wish He thanked us, but like one who paid little attention to what we said He appeared unsettled sometimes rising, —traversing the room, and then resuming his seat Lady Darnley called Louisa —She left us He still continued his silent mood I had neither spirits or inclination to break into it —I took my work, unpinned

unpinned it, and rolled it up again. He left the chair where he had been fitting, and took one next me—he seemed going to speak—nay, absolutely once did attempt to do so, but only heaved a deep sigh. I felt a confciousness some how, which prevented my asking him if he were well —Still we were both silent.

I lifted my eyes, to take one more view of the face I was so soon to be deprived of, again he was gazing on me. I haftily dropped mine to the ground—The chaife drove to the door—he started up—" O Caroline!" with a look that ran through my veins, and a heavy sigh——he uttered no more, but hurried out of the room, ere I could, if the power of speech had been left, have articulated one word.—I remained nailed to my chair—a cold trembling feized my limbs, my temples beat as if my head would fly in pieces. Soon after Harriot came into the room, and roused me from my *reverie.* She told me her brother was gone, and hardly took leave of any one. " For fo fhort an absence," faid I, " perhaps he did not think it necessary, or may be he dislikes taking leave as much as I do."

" I do not know," replied fhe, " but I thought it very odd. I met him in the lobby, he did not fay any thing——but his countenance difcovere.

——" What, what!" in a hefitating hurry I was going to fay, did his countenance difcover but checked myfelf. " what, did he not fpeak, fay you?" " No, only anfwered to my queftion, if he was going,——but I am fure he looked uneafy. I wanted to afk him fifty queftions, but he hurried into the chaife, and was bowled away in a moment."

* * *

Another letter from Mrs Grafton. Were I to give way to my fears, I fhould not open it till
hour

hour. But can she revoke what she before promised? Ah, no! Is she not the best of women? I will inclose it for your perusal.

* * *

Well, I suppose, you have read this dear welcome letter. Ah! what infinite obligations have I to the revered writer! Would to Heaven I could repay her tenderness, by laying before her my whole heart!——but it is impossible. Ah! into what a fatal snare has love drawn me! How I detest insincerity——and yet pursue it. It cannot now be avoided.——False delicacy involves us in a thousand difficulties, which once immersed in, it is not always in our power to extricate ourselves from.

This letter has given me inexpressible satisfaction, as it will enable me to act according to my own sentiments, with respect to Mr Davenport, who is, you know, to be here to-day. I will act openly with him, at least as openly as my heart will allow me; I will shew him both the letters I have received from Mrs. Grafton, upon his account, and the copy of mine to her.——I will likewise shew them to Lady Darnley. They will, I hope, satisfy her ladyship; for certainly she cannot think I will sacrifice my happiness to her punctilio, when my dear benefactress has given me leave unconditionally to reject Mr Davenport.

I cannot, I own, intirely acquit myself of injustice in treating Mr Davenport with so much civility last time he was here.——the motive too not a laudable one——not that I exceeded the common rules of good-breeding, but a vain man takes every little attention as a mark of distinction. I certainly acted wrong, and I condemn myself for it,——nor have I any excuse, but a bad one, I doubt.——Only people under the influence of a head-

head-strong-passion, cannot always answer for their taking the most prudent measures. But who then, you say, knowingly and aforethought would plunge themselves into these exigencies——apprised of the consequences? Ah! who indeed, but such silly weak folks as

Your

CAROLINE MELMOTH.

Thank Heaven, Davenport has sent an excuse. Something has prevented him——Of consequence too. I wish this affair of consequence required his attendance in the East-Indies, or any where else from hence and me.

LETTER XXXIX.

To Miss VERE.

Darnley-Grove, July 18.

DAVENPORT's excuse was only a respite, not a reprieve; for this day he paid us a visit. I hope it will be the last.

How do you think the man was engaged? With lawyers, my dear——absolutely with lawyers, making a settlement for me——Did you ever hear of such a proceeding?—Still without hope. But then to be sure, this last generous act was to work wonders in his behalf on my grateful heart. —No, no, my good Machiavel,—you were wrong in your conjectures, I give you my word—Yet this is owing to the politeness of my behaviour to him. He shall not again be led into the same error.

I shewed

I shewed Lady Darnley, and the young ladies, the letters I before mentioned; they were vastly pleased with that mark of my confidence. "I assured them, I had great obligations to them, for their kind intentions of making me happy, tho' they had failed in the method. The highest felicity I could flatter myself in receiving, was the continuance of their friendship, which it should be my chief endeavour never to forfeit by an unworthy action, of which I should ever think myself guilty, were I not the next opportunity to give Mr Davenport such a decisive answer, as should prevent any further solicitation from that quarter. I likewise begged Lady Darnley would use her influence over him, to engage him to desist from a pursuit, which rendered me unhappy, and which could never be of advantage to him."

She "promised to acquaint him with what I had said."

"It will be better, Madam, if you please, that I should not see Mr Davenport, were he to come."

"Why not," said Harriot, "surely you can best inform him of your own sentiments."

"Mr Davenport, my dear Miss Harriot, wants delicacy, in my opinion. I think, were I a man, I should cease to solicit any woman, when I found she had an invincible dislike to me, tho' I had loved her ever so well before; nay, for that very reason,—true love seeks the happiness of the object beloved; self in that case is totally absorbed, and only the desire of pleasing left."

"Well supported indeed," cried Harriot, "for one unacquainted with the *belle passion*."

"We often understand the theory, without being acquainted with the practice, you know," returned I, smiling. "I am only declaring the sentiments,

sentiments, I should imagine, would actuate the breast of a man of honor, who truly loved"

"Well, well, my dear," pursued Harriot, "you have strange delicate sentiments---I wish you may meet with a man worthy of them"

"I hope I need not travel far---I dare say, you could name several of your acquaintance"-

"Not I, I don't scrutinize so closely,---few, I believe, could bear the test"

Miss Cathcart called on us, to take a ride, which prevented our further conversation I must now attend the ladies in a walk, by appointment When I return, will continue my epistle, with the result of my conference with Mr Davenport

* * *

Well; to pursue my narrative in a methodical manner, I must inform you, on Wednesday Sir George left us, and on the present Friday, about an hour before the usual time of dinner, came Mr Davenport Lady Darnley thought proper to order dinner back, as she judged it the better way to have every thing adjusted between us as soon as possible

I intreated to be permitted to stay above stairs, but the ladies gave it unanimously against me

Down I went, accompanied by them After the customary salutations, Mr Davenport approached me, "apologized for his not recollecting an engagement of the last importance, which prevented him the great pleasure he had intended himself, but hoped it had not been the occasion of retarding any scheme we might have formed'

"Indeed it did, Sir," said I, "Lady Darnley had kindly promised us a very agreeable jaunt, before she received the honor of your card But it is to her ladyship, Sir, you should make your apologies"

"Ah!

"Ah! Madam," said he, sighing, "I feel the higheſt reſpect for Lady Darnley, and infinite compunction in being in the leaſt guilty of a ſoleciſm in good breeding.—But," added he, sighing ſtill deeper—and ſoftening his voice, his hand ſpread on his breaſt, "what torments await the unhappy man, who has offended you! and I ſee too plainly I am that wretch."

"Lord, Sir," cried I, looking at, or rather meaſuring him with my eyes,——"do you take me for the head of an inquiſition? Torments! and offence! I muſt feel a very great partiality for a man, before I think him of conſequence enough to be offended at him."

"Miſs Melmoth," ſaid Lady Darnley gravely, "you do not treat Mr Davenport in the politeſt terms."—Then turning to the man with the utmoſt gentleneſs, as if ſhe meant to apologize for my harſhneſs "You ſeemed, Sir, as if going to favor us with the reaſon which prevented us the pleaſure of ſeeing you."

"Madam," anſwered Mr Davenport, "I had appointed two gentlemen of the law to come from London. They arrived the very morning I had intended to come hither. The buſineſs they came upon kept me till afternoon; their part of it was not finiſhed 'till this morning. I thought, when I did come, it was beſt to bring my excuſe along with me," taking out a parchment from his pocket, "which, if my dear Miſs Melmoth will make me ſo happy as to accept, I would not exchange ſituations with an Eaſtern emperor." With this mellifluous ſpeech, putting one knee to the ground, his ſpread hand as uſual, the other flouriſhingly preſented the parchment to me. Thoſe we love not ever are ungraceful. The two Miſs Darnleys roſe, as if to go. Lady Darnley too
was

was moving "Stay, Madam," faid I, "my dear ladies, be fo kind as not to leave me. Mr Davenport can have nothing to fay to me, which you and all the world may not hear. I intreat you, Sir, to rife. Your pofture is unbecoming both yourfelf and me."

"Are you then cruelly refolved to fee me expire at your feet? Inhuman, inexorable- -lovely Caroline! But," rifing, "you muft and ever fhall be obeyed by me."

"If my commands had any weight with you, Sir, you would leave perfecuting me in this manner. As to your fettlement---" for he had fpread open the parchment in fuch a way, that I could not avoid feeing it, without affectedly turning away my eyes ---He afterwards fhewed it intirely to Lady Darnley. It was twelve hundred a year for my fole and feparate ufe---" As to your fettlement, Sir, I muft fay, notwithftanding your motive, it is noble, and like yourfelf. Permit me, Sir, to emulate your generous behaviour, and by acting equally generous, fave you the mortification and myfelf the guilt of joining myfelf to you. I have but little to beftow. My heart alone could give that little, value. Surely then, my heart ought to be his who receives my vows! Your's it can never be. Do not then urge me further, I befeech you, Sir. Here is the letter which Mr, Grafton wrote me after you had given yourfelf the trouble——needlefs trouble, allow me, Sir, to call it, as you then was no ftranger to my fentiments—to go up to London. This, Sir, is the copy of my anfwer, and this the reply. Pardon me, Sir, but if I know my own heart, I know I can never retract what I have faid. Call me not obftinate or inexorable. I hope I have convinced you, you

could

could not find any happiness in a connection with me. I likewise hope sincerely, the next lady you honor with your addresses, may be sensible of your merit, and have a free undivided heart to bestow, which I"—I paused, but presently recovered myself, tho' it cost me a sigh—" which I make no doubt you soon will. I shall be very glad to hear you are happy. And when you have experienced the felicity of a mutual attachment, you will readily thank me for my sincerity, tho' you are not yet able to do it. I am very sorry for the uneasiness you have had on my account, but I have not been without my share. Ladies, I beg your pardons, for having thus intruded on your patience —Permit me to withdraw." I arose, and courtesying to each respectfully, retired to my apartment.

I really pitied poor Davenport. He looked like a statue during my long harangue. He bowed to my compliment, but spoke not a word.

Louisa followed me up stairs. She found me in tears.

" Tell me," said I, " is Lady Darnley displeased with me?"

" No my dear," answered she, " who can blame you? But my Caroline, why in tears? Why these soft drops of sorrow? If you have acted according to your sentiments and approved judgment, why should you be afflicted?"

" I know not," said I, wiping them away, and sighing. " I am convinced I acted as I ought. How base it would have been in me to have taken advantage of Mr Davenport's weakness for me! But I cannot bear to give pain to any one. My heart always suffers in proportion to the anguish it occasions; yet I could not consent to make myself for ever miserable, which must have been my lot with Mr Davenport. We know too well the

VOL I   I   horrid

horrid situation of one, who is devoted to the person, their aversion."

"Too true!" said Louisa, with a sigh the tears starting in her eyes, tho' she strove to conceal them "Such a situation must be dreadful——I do not blame you—Who can?

' Parted from those we love, what harder fate?
Why harder far to live with those we hate."

At this juncture, Harriot came in, " Lord, my dear," said she to me, " by that melancholy phiz, I should have thought you had just parted from a beloved lover, instead of having been discarding a despised one But come, won't you go down? My mother will never be able to prevail on your dejected and rejected swain to stay dinner Upon my word he is a perfect Orlando Furioso But go down, and try if your influence can prevail on him, to relinquish his scheme of hanging himself on a willow, or casting his listless length at the foot of it, and augmenting the streams with his briny tears."

"No, my dear," said I, " I cannot think of going down Excuse me, I am not able at present to answer your raillery If I were to go down to intreat Mr Davenport to stay, it would look as if I were capable of triumphing over the distresses of my fellow-creatures I arrogate none to myself, in that I have been the occasion of pain (tho' innocently so) nor will I wear the appearance of it."

"You are a very good, and a very extraordinary girl, Caroline"

"Not so extraordinary, I hope, Harriot"—smiling.

"I rather

"I rather hope you are ex-tra-or-di-nary tho' For if you are not, I shall be very much reduced indeed, for hang me, if I should not feel a little exultation upon such an occasion. I know it would be wrong---aye, infinitely wrong, so you need not put on that look of astonishment, as if I did not know wrong from right, but neverthelefs, I doubt I should. To have a fine young fellow suing for mercy at my feet, while I, his sovereign empress, held out the sceptre, or killed him with a frown, as should best please me, tho' I believe I should do the last, to shew my power, and to strike terror in the rest of the wretches."

"Since you promise yourself so much pleasure in discarding lovers, why do you retain so many in your service? and how do you reconcile this seeming inconsistency?"

"O, why, I don't know. Why among all my fellows, there is not one who would feel half so much pain, or look half so woe-begone as your enamorato. And I have no notion of lessening my train for nothing neither."

"Then pray turn off one, and take Davenport in his room. What say you? I dare say, if you play off an eye-battery---as you once called it--- against him, you may bring the governor to terms."---"Of capitulation," interrupted she, "and that would spoil all. No I shall leave him to the willow-tree, or the babbling brook, whichever seemeth best in his eyes."

"Well then, since we have both done with Mr Davenport, tell me your candid opinion of him."

"Why, my candid opinion is, that two-thirds of the women of my acquaintance would call him a pretty-fellow, and be immensely happy to be distinguished

distinguished by him in public! Nay, many would pull caps for him, and hardly one refuse him for an husband. This, my dear, is the most forceable plea I can use against his not being capable of pleasing you. Your ideas are rather particular —— Amazingly different from most of the modern Misses, who, no doubt, would think you altogether outré."

"I am glad, however, I have your approbation."

"Aye, aye, child, you have it, if that does you any honor.—But see,—behold, as I live, your swain is off—absolutely gone, Caroline; your lover is flown."

"Thank God! and I hope never to return in that character again. Now I will attend you down."

"Pray do, for I am very hungry.——I cannot live upon love. Poor Davenport has lost the substance by catching at the shadow. Indeed you should have let the poor man have made a good dinner first. I doubt he has lost his stomach, as well as his labor."

"Unmerciful girl, thus to trifle with another's pain!"

"I was not the cause of it, Caroline," archly.

"Nor did I wish to be so, Harriot."

By this time we reached the dining-room. Lady Darnley and Louisa were there. "Am I so unhappy as to have incurred your ladyship's disapprobation?"

"No, my dear," answered Lady Darnley, taking my hand, "I approve your conduct. Mr Davenport too, tho' a great sufferer, cannot condemn your explicitness. You certainly deserve commendation in not suffering interest to bias you, when

when your heart could allow no favor to Mr Davenport."

Happy was I to have this troublesome affair so well over, I feel quite a new creature. So relieved. But ah! how many, many degrees from happiness!——Happiness did I say? From ease.

Mr Davenport has so engaged my thoughts, that they had hardly time to dwell on any thing else. But now they continually revert to the dear object which engrosses my whole soul. "O Caroline!" still does the sound vibrate on my ear—still do I see the look which accompanied the exclamation.

Lady Darnley by her kind behaviour seemed to take a load off my breast. I appeared quite cheartul while at dinner, and when it was over, I went to the harpsicord. I sung and played. in short the latter part of the day passed sweetly.

I will now releate my dear Sidney. I receive, by intuition, your congratulations on my so happily extricating myself from the *embarras* of Mr Davenport.

Farewel, my dear; and believe me faithfully

Your's

Caroline Melmoth.

LETTER XL.

To Miss Vere.

Darnley-Grove, July 12.

I AM not very well, nor in good spirits; but that you will tell me is no news. I have time to write a long letter—if I find matter for it——

as Lady Darnley and her daughters are gone out this afternoon, to pay a visit in the *environs* As they are strangers to me, I got excused, having a most cruel head-ach my heart not in a better state A whole week elapsed, and no Sir George Yet why should I wish him to be here ? I tell my self continually, I ought to rejoice in his absence I tell myself so, but all my sophistry does not con vince me No ——I had rather remain in the same delusive error I see my folly, but cannot wish to be wise

I have spent an hour in the picture-gallery, con templating the portrait of a certain amiable man by Reynolds —I seated myself opposite to it, and fixed my eyes, 'till they were incapable of dif tinguishing the lovely form I dried them,—— and sighed Again I gazed ——Again I wept At last my reflections became too keen, and I retired to my closet Not to write——I had not eyes for some time

It is madness, thus to indulge myself, and I know it I form a thousand resolutions in a mo ment, and break them as fast as I form them Ah! why do I not take the only method left me— Flight My visit has already been a long one But I cannot propose it to Mrs Grafton, to lay her commands on me to quit Darnley-Grove, and un less she does, they declare they will not part with me

Ah! did Lady Darnley know my heart, as you do, she would want no inducement to send me away How would she contemn the earth born creature!

Pshaw,—an interruption To ask me if I will drink tea in my dressing-room, or in the saloon — Where-ever they please It would look particular, or I would not take any this afternoon I have no
inclination

inclination to quit my pen I will in the evening take a ftrole in the park, perhaps the air may relieve the intolerable pain in my head Where fhall I find the remedy for my other pains?

My God, Sidney! What chaife is that? Frederic! As I live, Sir George!—Heavens fupport me! He was not expected This fudden furprife has overcome me ——What a filly weak creature I am! I can hardly hold my pen—Thefe lines— I could almoft wifh he had not come—His myfterious air, when laft we parted——What fhall I do with him?——I muft go down Alone too —— Lord blefs me! I muft go down He does not know I have feen him. My ftaying only encreafes my perturbation Would to Heaven—I do not know what I would fay Adieu.

In Continuation

O Sidney, how fhall I begin? how find words to recount ha'f the tranfports of my foul? No: words are too weak. I am all ecftacy—joy and love Yes Sidney, let me repeat,——all love. But let me lead to the enchanting fcene.

In a thoufand terrors, of I know-not-what, I went down ftairs into the drawing-room I had been there but a little time, when Sir George entered He afked after my health, in a hefitating manner I, in no calmer way, made my inquiries We fat down 'Tea was brought in. We fipped it in filence, except now and then a trifling queftion, which being anfwered on both fides, by monofyllables, confequently finifhed each fubject, as foon as begun

When the things were removed, and the fervant retired, an awful paufe continued. At length, without

without speaking, Sir George rose, and traversed the room his countenance pale and dejected, as I could see in one of the pier glasses. He continued walking some time. At last, after several fruitless attempts, I assumed courage enough to open my lips "You are not well, I fear, Sir George."

"No, madam, nor shall I ever be so"—with a deep sigh.

"I am sorry to hear you say so, Sir George," I could not help re-echoing his sigh my eyes cast down.

"Can you be sorry for me?" replied he, stepping up quick to me, with a softened air. Then turning from me, "What signifies your sorrow?" ——Immediately clasping his hands, he exclaimed "O happy, happy Davenport!"

I trembled all over, and was ready to faint In a broken voice and sounds, scarcely articulate, I prayed Sir George to explain himself. "Forgive me, Caroline," said he, throwing himself at my feet, "forgive me, but I must for ever adore you."

"Gracious powers!" exclaimed I, "Is it possible? Am I so blest?" I could say no more. Nor did I need, you will think I spoke plain enough But it is impossible to tell you all. Suffice it to say, I find myself beloved by the most amiable of men. Never did any man express more rapture; at least, I never was so sensible of it in any man.

Such floods of joy pour in upon my heart, I can hardly give utterance to it. He has told me all his sufferings I have not been much inferior to him in that article.

It was some time before we could descend from our altitudes, and talk like reasonable beings When we had a little reduced our conversation to the

the level of common sense, I observed, as Sir George was sitting by me, holding one of my hands, the other fondly thrown round my waist—I observed, I say, his waistcoat being open at the breast,———a sight that alarmed me exceedingly,—no other than the little picture I once mentioned to you. The recollection of the anguish it occasioned me, caused me to sigh. How attentive is true love! " Why that sigh, my adorable Caroline ? Has my love any doubts ? Suffer your Darnley to clear them. Tell me, my sweet girl " His dear eyes expressive of the utmost tenderness.

I would have evaded an answer; but Sir George again intreated. I then said, with a melancholy I could not conceal, I fancy there is some happy woman nearer the heart of my amiable Darnley, than his poor Caroline."

" Unkind, cruel Caroline, what could suggest so strange an idea ?" " At least," said I, " the resemblance of one is " at the same time throwing my eyes upon it. He followed their direction, and taking it from the ribbon on which it hung, and pressing it to his lips,—" Behold," said he, " my only consolation. This has been my constant companion. Look on it, my love, nor wonder, that I placed it next my heart, where the bright original has reigned so long " He presented it to me. Ah, Sidney! it was my own picture.
" But I wonder" said I, " how you could possibly procure my likeness."

" I will explain it to you," rejoined Sir George. " You remember once at St. James's-Square, Lord F. proposed a game at questions and commands. You seemed inattentive, and paid many forfeits, among which, was a small shagreen case. I received it with perturbation, and took the ear-left opportunity of quitting the room I eagerly opened it, not without the greatest apprehension, that it might be same happy favored lover How great was my joy, when I discovered the perfect resemblance of my angel! I pressed it to my lips in a transport, when a thought started into my mind Immediately it was put in execution I sent to Meyers with proper instructions, and the strictest charges of care. I then returned to the company, and renewed my office of forfeit-keeper Fortunately you did not demand the restitution of the shagreen case; you know what excuses I made to you, when you did Meyers executed his commission amazingly well, there was no difference to be discovered. However, I returned you the copy, as I was more flattered in keeping that, for which you really had sat It has never been from my bosom, there it has ever hung, and there it shall remain"

Ah! my beloved Sidney, do you think I was not delighted? It is impossible to tell you how much I was

I could not help hinting, it grew late,——and if Lady Darnley should surprise us, knowing, as we both did, her sentiments—it would be the better way to separate

He owned the justice of my advice, but said, " How can I possibly take it? I am but as it were this moment become acquainted with felicity, but just tasted life Can you, from whom these blessings spring, wish to deprive me so early of them, by urging me to lose sight of your beauties? The body could as easily exist without the soul, as adoring Darnley without his Caroline "

" But you see the necessity, my dear Sir George,—and I shall see you again soon."

" Take

"Take but one turn with me in the garden, then, and I will obey you in every thing you command"

I accompanied him in a walk How beautiful did every shrub appear! each flower seemed conscious of delight Ah! how different from my late walks was this! All was harmony, and love The birds too joined to congratulate us, I thought I felt a general philanthropy from my particular happiness My Darnley too! Amiable, charming creature! Is it really true?——am I beloved by him?—All seems a pleasing *rêverie*

He has made me promise to rise early to-morrow morning, and meet him in the park. I cannot refuse him—tho' perhaps I ought.

July 24.

I have had a most delightful ramble in the park this morning, which you will be very well able to account for

Our conversation was very interesting, tho' too long to repeat It is so common to say, the discourse of lovers will not bear a repetition, that I will not make it here

I feel myself infinitely happy but still a thousand fears will intrude Yet I hardly know what becomes of them, when my Darnley smiles.—— But obstacles innumerable still remain, tho' love contrives to throw a mist over our eyes, or rather, we shut them to conviction

I recounted to Sir George part of the humiliating conversation I had with Lady Darnley, but Sir George will endeavour to persuade me, she will overlook every trifling disadvantage to make us happy.

"I told him I was so, in finding myself beloved by him. That now we were convinced of the sincerity

sincerity of our affection to each other, we should stop there. The discovery he had made yesterday, would in itself afford me a lasting satisfaction,—nor would I suffer myself to wish for more. It was madness to think Lady Darnley would ever give her consent, to unite such a one as me to her family, and my resolution was never to injure any of it by a procedure, which must bring down everlasting and deserved contempt upon my head."

"Nor will I ever urge you to a procedure, which shall call forth the slightest blush. I have, my dearest Caroline, a very great love and respect for my mother, I know her to be a valuable woman.—and the only shade in the most amiable character, is that unfortunate family-pride. She cannot divest herself of that fatal prepossession—that great and virtuous deeds can only be expected from noble birth, tho' they are sometimes found in the plebeian kind. I own, I have often beheld with the utmost surprise, the tender affection she bears you, which plainly indicates, she can see, and acknowledge your shining merit, unaccompanied by noble birth, and hereditary riches. If, under these, to my mother—great disadvantages, you have gained her esteem, she will the less wonder her son is not insensible to it."

"Lady Darnley and my sisters have often pressed me to marry. Highly as they know I esteem that state, they must have remarked the invincible coolness I have ever discovered, when they have mentioned any lady to me. They wish to see me happy. I know, I possess their love——And when they see there is but one way, and one woman to make me so, my mother will not, I dare hope, refuse her concurrence."

"I am so far of Rousseau's opinion, the child owes obedience to the parent, no longer than it is
under

under their care, a duty and respect it ever owes ——such I will ever pay I will never marry to make my mother unhappy,—but at the same time," kissing my hand, " I will never relinquish the dear hope of calling you mine I will endeavour to wait with patience, till I find an opportunity of disclosing my attachment, with certainty of success, to my mother, in the mean time, I need not advise my adorable Caroline to conciliate as much as possible Lady Darnley's favor Her increasing esteem will render every thing as we wish."

Thus in sweet converse the hours fled away Already we had been together three hours Nor did we at all find ourselves fatigued, or thought the time tedious We were seated by a most delightful fall of water on one side, on the other, a noble grove, which extends from the house, and gives its name to it,

Whose deep imbow'ring shade
Seems form'd for love, and contemplation made

A thousand birds tuning their little throats to harmony Before us, a most extensive view of hills and dales, hanging woods and waving corn-fields I have sat upon this very seat, to be sure, twenty times since I have been here, but its beauties never struck me before,——or I was incapable of tasting them. Joined to this heavenly scene around us, figure to yourself, your Caroline, her dear amiable Darnley by her side—and then, if you ever loved fervently and mutually, you may form an adequate idea of my inexpressible felicity

We were interrupted in the midst of our discourse, when we thought we had not said half enough,

enough, by the clock ſtriking nine. As that is the hour the ladies generally make their appearance, we thought it beſt to proceed to the houſe. At ſome little diſtance we ſeparated, as it would have furniſhed matter of ſpeculation, had we been ſeen to come in together

How different is Sir George Darnley's aſpect now, to what it was! His mother and ſiſters congratulated him upon his perfect amendment I endeavour to avoid his looks as much as poſſible,— Indeed I hardly ever ſuffer my eyes to wander, where yet they are too willing to ſtray

I ſhall tire you, my dear Sidney, with dull repetitions, but you were partaker of my woes,— ſhall you not then equally participate in my true felicity?

The —— Aſſembly is next week Sir George, would be willing to go, but ſays, he fears he muſt not dance with me, and he ſhall not eaſily ſupport the ſight of any aſſiduous happy coxcomb, fluttering about and entertaining me

"Not entertaining me, Sir George," ſaid I, looking at him with tender delight, "you have put it out of the power of any man to entertain me But I can eaſily prevent any diſagreeableneſs to you, by not dancing

"Dear creature," replied he, "and would you, to humour your Darnley, deprive yourſelf of the triumph you ſo juſtly claim over half your ſex"

"My only triumph will be in the hope of pleaſing you, Sir George."

"Heaven make me worthy of your goodneſs, my beloved Caroline, and I ſhall be the happieſt of men!"

And I, of women, I am ſure, Sidney! I wiſh you were here to partake my happineſs,——and yet,

yet, it is not without allay. But away all doubts and tears——every solicitude——Darnley loves me, and while I am possessed of his heart, I will not give way to an unpleasing idea. I forget I was ever unhappy! I feel so light, so tranquil. Ah! had he but the sanction of Lady Darnley, to justify his choice, the happiest of all beings would then be

Your

Caroline Melmoth

LETTER XLI.

To William Stanhope, Esq,

Darnley-Grove, July 27.

STANHOPE, your late dejected friend is now the happiest fellow in the universe. How is this, you will cry—What, is it possible the sighing lover has shook off his chains? No. Nor would I part with them for the world's empire — I am impatient to draw them still closer.—But the dear enchanting angel loves me.—Ah! Stanhope, if ever you loved sincerely (which is a doubt with me,—for faith, I almost think no man ever loved as I do) you would, I say, be a judge of my ineffable delight, when almost reduced to despair —the lovely, adorable, blushing maid, owned she loved. How the dear sound vibrates on my ear!

She too has long sighed,—she feared, in vain. Ah! that I had sooner, by disclosing my passion, given relief to both our hearts!

I wish

I wish you were to see her: and yet it might be dangerous. I would ask you to come and see me, but am apprehensive.—No! you had better not.—Her charms might undo you, and I lose a friend. I know you would be my rival, but I would not ensure you success. No, that lovely blushing sincerity confirms my hopes.

Never woman inspired desire, admiration, and respect, as she does,—so sweetly blending tenderness, and maiden diffidence.

By Heaven! I never knew the joys of love before. Its pains I have long been acquainted with, but they are now all over.—How rapturous is the situation I am in with this lovely girl!

It is one of my sister Harriot's chief excellencies that she can see and acknowledge the beauty of my angel. I remember a conversation—indeed it sunk very deep in my memory, for many reasons. It was a family-piece, Lady Darnley, the two girls, and your friend, who was perusing a book, which however soon became of little use to me, only as it gave me a pretence not to join in it.

The conversation turned some how or other on beauty.

" Beauty," said Harriot, " is allowed to be nothing but in the lover's eye; I do not maintain that as my opinion: on the contrary, I affirm, when a happy assemblage of features unite in the face of man or woman, every spectator must take pleasure in beholding them, tho' they may not have the justice to own it. And among all the persons I know, whether male or female, I do not believe there is one that can behold Caroline Melmoth, for instance, without emotions; it may be envy you know in the breasts of the latter."

" Miss Caroline Melmoth," said my mother, " is very handsome to be sure."

" Handsome!"

"Handsome!" repeated Harriot, "she is an angelic creature."

"You speak with rapture, Harriot," said her sister, "it is well you are not a man."

"If I was," replied she, "I should certainly be over head and ears in love with her. I never beheld such eyes. And then her mouth—how pretty it is!—a thousand little dimples continually playing.—In short, I never yet saw so complete a set of features, arranged in so sweet a form, as we see in her face——Nay, her whole person is lovely.---Her disposition too, so engaging. She seems the only person in the world who is insensible of her numberless charms.---And were I a man, I would prefer Caroline Melmoth, as she is, to the first princess in the world."

"Then I am very happy, Harriot," said Lady Darnley, "you are my *daughter*---were you my *son*, I should tremble for you."

I had heard quite enough in this last speech, and more than I chose; therefore arose, saying,---
"It is utterly impracticable for a man to read in the company of ladies. I have not been able to attend to your discourse, or my book, and must finish my study in the library."

I went thither, but faith, not to study, unless it was the charms of my Caroline. Yes,---she shall be mine. My mother is exceedingly fond of her, and I shall leave it a little to time to effect the rest. It is impossible she can refuse her consent, when the happiness of a darling son is at stake; that son too, no way dependent upon her, tho' I pay her the utmost deference and respect.

All my inquietudes concerning Davenport, were wholly groundless. My lovely girl has suffered as much as I have on his account. I could almost pity

pity the poor fellow losing such a woman, was he capable of tasting her perfections; but such men marry fine women, rather to gratify their vanity, than any other passion. The next admired girl will do as well for him, as this lovely one destined for me

Harriot spoke truth, when she said, Caroline was the only person in the world insensible of her merit. She never arrogates any to herself, even for her acquired accomplishments. She speaks on any topic with the utmost perspicuity and judgment, but very seldom can be drawn out, thro' diffidence; such an unassumingness in her manner——so willing to be on the hearing side---so perfectly feminine, without the airs of our modern fine ladies, who expire at operas, or faint at the sight of a frog. Her judgment is found— I never heard her make an injudicious observation. Ever makes allowances for the failings of others, ——to herself, strictly rigid.

You will think, my dear Will, " I read her over with a lover's eye," but these were my remarks---and not mine alone---before I commenced one; for all lovely as she is, I did not at once submit to her powerful charms.

I saw her beautiful and engaging, but 'till my heart felt the soft influence of love, I had too much of the pride inherent to my family; but when the soft contagion seized my soul, my prudent scruples melted as the new-fallen summer-snow beneath a sun-beam, nor left a trace behind.

Absorbed in my passion, I owned no other power, nor ever shall, so amiable is the dear object of my affections, and I am naturally of a constant disposition I can never change. was my love indeed fixed only on her form, that might,
from

from possession, pall upon the sense, but the foundation of my love, is esteem, and sensibility of charms exceeding beauty. The mind stored with riches, as my Caroline's is, must afford variety to the most faithless of men.

You will tell me, my letter is immensely entertaining, and to enhance the pleasure you receive from the perusal, it is perfectly *nouvelle*. I beg your pardon, Stanhope, lovers have short memories——I have repeated all this to you a thousand times——you are no lover, or you would easily excuse me. I wish you were, as you can have no idea of the infinite happiness of a man, beloved by a lovely virtuous woman. You are, I know not why, not so delicate in your notions of women, as I am, if it is from experience of the sex——but I hope not——However say nothing, I charge you, to lessen it in my esteem.

I cannot think how you have lived a bachelor so long, if you have avoided any pain by it, you must own you have lost a thousand pleasures——— But I am throwing away time, to write to you of love; it is like consulting a blind man in the choice of colors,——for say what you will, you never yet have known any thing of that blessing,

" Which Heaven in our cup has thrown "

I shall break off here, for which, I suppose, you will render me your hearty thanks. It is near six, and the loveliest of women promised to meet me at that hour.

Adieu, Stanhope. I sincerely pity you, and all mankind.

GEORGE DARNLEY

LETTER

LETTER XLII.

To Miss Vere.

Darnley-Grove, July 30.

WHAT infinite pleasure did your dear letter * give me! Ah! you co-incide with my sentiments! How flattering to my hopes, your praises!——Sweet, as Cicero says, are the praises of those we love. Next to the delight of being beloved by the dear object, for whom we have sighed, is the concurrence of our friends.——My Sidney, the sister of my heart! approves my choice! It must, it must be fortunate.—Ah! that Lady Darnley——but it were madness at present ——He must not think of——or even wish it.— We have youth on our side. We must wait with patience, a season more propitious.

I am quite a different creature. I am now assured of his heart——I behold each day with new delight. No more do I spend the night in wakeful anxiety; pleasing reflections on the past day fill my mind, and sooth it to rest. My whole thoughts are fixed on the most amiable of men, and sink into gentle slumbers, where in dreams, he repeats the thousand fond things, a lover's eloquence renders so pleasing.

He has made me a present of his picture, a striking, tho' not flattered likeness——Ah! what need of flattery!—elegantly and richly set with brilliants.——Itself to me a jewel, above all price, no ornament surely necessary. With what joy I received this mark of his affection! It will be my only solace, in my lonely hours.——

We

---

* Miss Vere's letter does not appear.

We went to the assembly.——I chose not to dance, tho' much pressed. Mr. Davenport was there. I wished to avoid him.——He bowed very respectfully to all of us, and paid a slight compliment as he passed us.

After some time, Sir George brought a gentleman up to me, and begged I would go down one dance with him. " You will find this gentleman a very good dancer" said he, and added, in a whisper——" not unworthy your notice. Nor on him let Hebe once frown, tho' I cannot allow her to smile." He tenderly pressed my hand, and presented me to the gentleman, who led me to the sett. We stood next to him, so we had an opportunity of chatting very agreeably now-and-then. He told me, when at tea, that was his motive for requesting me to join the jovial crew—as he could not avoid dancing himself, and if he had, our both sitting down together, would be looked on as particular—nor did he know how to support my being absent from his sight so long.

Finding it agreeable to the only man I would wish to appear so to, I continued dancing as long as the rest of the company.——My partner was a very agreeable man, who did not talk nonsense by wholesale, as most of our petit-maitres do.

How very different were my sensations now, to what they were when I saw Sir George engaged *tête à tête* with Miss Featherstone! What did I not endure the last time!

But my heart is now entirely at rest.—Perhaps, you will call my security—vanity, but I have not now the least tincture of jealousy in my composition. It may, in some degree, be owing to the good opinion Sir George has given me of myself; I assure you, I begin to think very tolerably of my abilities. When did I otherwise, you ask—

memento

memento your converfation with Lady Darnley
Ah! why did I revive that difagreeable circum
ftance?—Avaunt, I will not fuffer my mind to
dwell upon it

Do you not exprefs fome curiofity to know how
the poor rejected Davenport looked, and behaved?
——Amazing, Sidney! you are not a female, fure!
—Nay, if you are fo indifferent, I fhall not attempt it—You fuppofe it, you fay.——Well, do
fo if you will, it will fave me a great deal of
trouble He is going to an eftate he has in Lan-
cafhire—there to mourn and lament his cruel dif-
appointment I hope I fhall never more have occafion to mention his name, fo thus concludes the
hiftory of the gentleman and the fettlement

* * *

We went two days ago to a country-wake——
Sir George gave us all fairings——we did the fame;
——fuch as the place would afford. We fpent a
very pleafant day

He has got a new phaeton down, very elegant,
very high, and quite the thing He invited one
of us to take an airing with him in it, his fifters
both objected to the accompanying him, thro'
fear he afked me, if I fhould be afraid to ven-
ture I anfwered, "I apprehended, if there were
danger, he would not make the offer." "Well
then," faid Harriot, do you and Caroline whifk
away with your four prancing hunters, while
Louifa and I will ride on horfeback, that, with our
attendants, we may be ready to affift you, in cafe
of accidents."

We were foon equipped for our little excurfion
——and a moft delightful one it was to me Sir
George told me, he fent for the equipage on purpofe to have an opportunity of converfing with
me,

me, as his fisters had frequently expressed their dislike to phaetons ——What an artful creature!

We spent the day at a delightfully-charming retreat, small, but infinitely pleasant. About ten miles from Darnley-Grove, and belongs to one of the tenants. The prospect one the most inviting that can be conceived.

Sir George proposed coming one day next week; Lady Darnley to be of the party. The fair sisters will attend her ladyship in the post-chaise.

Miss Darnley, who is very fond of riding on horseback, proposed, that we should frequently make little expeditions. Who could make an objection? Not I, I am sure. If I did, it must have been a very faint one.

You will hardly think we are prudent in promoting, or at least giving into these schemes, as it may breed suspicion, but you will cease to wonder, when I tell you, we have not a moment in which we can exchange a look or word——except two or three times that I have met him in the morning. What need, you will say, of speaking every moment? You are now assured of his affections, can it be necessary for him to tell you so every moment? Why no. And yet, Sidney, love, under these restrictions, is an inexhaustible fund. The repetition never tires.—There is always something new to say upon the subject.

I fancy, you wish I could find something new to say. You are fatigued with the same dull story. I am now going to take the morning air, which, however, will produce nothing new, I fear.

* * *

Twelve o'Clock.
Ah Sidney! what will become of me?—Good God! an express just arrived from London.—My
dear

dear benefactress perhaps no more ———I repeat, what will become of the forlorn Caroline?———A fit!—Poor, dear, good woman! Heaven preserve the worthiest, best of her sex!—I know not what I write—I am half distracted She could not die without seeing her child —Ah! my amiable, my kind guardian, your child flies to pay her dutiful respects to you.

Merciful God, grant her to my prayers! Abridge my days, and add them to the life of the ornament of thy works

A tap at the door It is my Darnley He is come to take a melancholy leave of me He could not do it before witnesses ———How kindly, how tenderly, he confoled me! Ah! could he think my tears flowed from a selfish motive?—Is then my filial love, a mercenary love!

No, I can never doubt your sincerity, best of men. I will believe, no change of circumstances can occasion one in you.

But the chaise is ready —I come this moment ———I must send this unfinished letter to the post office—Will write as foon as I get to town Ah! should I arrive too late, what a lasting affliction would it prove to your distressed

CAROLINE MELMOTH

LETTER XLIII

To Sir GEORGE DARNLEY, in answer to Letter XLI

Wellborough, July 30

MY dear George, your epistle—it is much too heroic to be styled a letter—is the perfect epitome of a man in love. But I do not
wonder

wonder at you, it is now your feafon. Only that a lover can never attend to reafon, I think I could fubmit fome things to your judgment, which, were it not will-o-wifp'd-away by love, might have fome weight

In your prefent attachment to Mifs Melmoth, I fee my former one to Charlotte Greville. She had all the charms in my eyes, which your Caroline poffeffes in yours! and I, all the love glowing in my heart—notwithftanding your doubts—which you have painted in your letter

But why do I harrow up my foul with the recollection of former pain?—Yet it is for your fake I tear open my wounds. I would endeavour to convince you—of what I know you will think an impoffibility—the almoft certainty of every woman proving falfe. Intereft is their God. Is it not owing to experience of the vileft perfidy in woman, I have drawn a too juft character of the whole fex? You have faid, I am not a friend to them—The man lives not, that had a higher opinion of them——but my efteem was founded in my ignorance. my knowledge taught me this leffon—never to truft a woman, whofe intereft it being to appear to love me, might wear the femblance of paffion to deceive me.

Believe me, my dear Darnley, no gratitude can bind the fex. Surely I had as much reafon to expect faithfulnefs as any man.—But, like too many men, I was deceived

You love to diftraction, Darnley; and therefore, love without prudence.—You dwell with pleafure on your fifter's attachment and commendations of your angel——You, no doubt, think yourfelf the more fecure, becaufe it is faid, women beft know one another.—may you never be deceived in your fancied fecurity!

If I make you angry by my freedom, I shall be extremely sorry, but my friendship must plead my excuse. I should be likewise sorry, if you were to draw any conclusions from my inferences, to the prejudice of Miss Melmoth, she may be an exception to the too general rule. Yet, Darnley, permit me to ask you one question. Would not any woman, guided and impelled by interest alone, act just as this lady has done?——By the accounts you have given me of Miss Melmoth, her birth is doubtful——her fortune precarious. I am afraid, hereafter, were you to marry her, you would repent of it. It is plain, from all you have ever said to me, notwithstanding the favor shewn her by the ladies of your family, they never thought of her as a relation in any other light, I presume, *you* would not think of her, and in that, I think, you ought not. Even if Lady Darnley could be brought to consent, which it would be madness to flatter yourself with—I repeat, you ought not to think of her.

It is a just observation, that they alone condemn the pride of ancestry, who have no family to boast of. Is it not a pleasing reflection that so many of our family have gone before us, worthy of being remembered by posterity? No one on earth has a higher idea of these sentiments than your mother. She, who could look with contempt on a duke descended unlawfully from a king, can never surely concur with your wishes. tho' an only son perhaps too, for that reason, are you not the guardian of your family's honor?

I know you are a man of honor, or these dissuasives from matrimony would be useless, as then your heart would have suggested an easier method of attaining the summit of your wishes. But you are a man infinitely more likely to be deceived,

than

than to deceive, which is no imputation on your judgment, but a proof of the real goodness of your heart On that, I depend for my acquittal.

I believe you will not think my arguments conclusive, in your situation perhaps I should not. However you conduct yourself, I hope you will have nothing to condemn yourself for Adieu, my dear George.

I am faithfully your's

Wm Stanhope

LETTER XLIV

To Miss Vere

Grosvenor Square, Aug 2

WITH travelling all night post, I arrived yesterday Thank Heaven! my dearest guardian is something better, tho' still in danger. She thought so herself, as she made some alterations and additions to her will Ah! may it be long, ere there is occasion for opening it!

When I entered the room, and approached her, she reached out her hand "Is it my Caroline? then I can die content" I knelt by the bed-side, and taking her hand, bathed it with my tears. —Words were not at my command

Miss Grafton in my mind makes rather a parade with her grief, however, people are differently affected, I believe I am sure, I feel as much affliction as it is possible a heart naturally tender, and sensible of the highest obligations from my more than parent, can feel but my grief is mute, whereas, Miss Grafton cries and laments aloud,—nay, sometimes disturbs her aunt, by her violent

violent affliction. You will think me ill-natured, when I say, I fear there is a little affectation in this vehement sorrow ——or perhaps she may,—conscious of not paying all the respect due to her aunt—be apprehensive of not sharing her fortune. I hope however she is not so mercenary.

I wanted to watch by my dearest friend last night, but Miss Grafton would by no means suffer me, "lest I should injure my health after my fatigue, both of body and mind, besides, if I did sit up, she must do so likewise, as she could not think of taking rest while her dear aunt was in such imminent danger." I was horridly provoked with her, for saying so much before Mrs Grafton.

"I told her, she was very unfit to attend any one in sickness, as she lowered their spirits."

She answered, "she could not conceal her sensibility."——Would you have suspected Miss Grafton of tenderness, my dear Sidney?

My fatigue indeed was very great, having had no rest for eight and thirty hours, and quick travelling, hardly waiting for any refreshment, as we had horses ready at every stage,——owing to the prudent forethought of Sir George Darnley, who dispatched the express back, to order relays for me.

I am now going to my dear benefactress, will at present bid you adieu.

In Continuation
August 3d.

Mrs Grafton continues on the mending hand, ——the Doctors pronounce her out of danger. How sincerely did my heart rejoice at their assurances!

I think it rather odd of Miss Grafton, she strives to prevent my being so frequently in her aunt's aunt's room, as I would wish. One time, she makes an excuse, that she is asleep, or some trifling thing or other continually, which however I heed not. Then she is so assiduous in taking every thing to Mrs. Grafton,——so doubly diligent, to use the expression——so very different to what she used to be, yet exceedingly polite to me. I really think, she often makes Mrs. Grafton worse by her talking to her. She will put a thousand insignificant questions to her, which, trivial as they are, still require answers.

Miss Grafton and I were sitting after supper last night in the dining-room, when she began a conversation, which, I own, rather amazed me. "Do you know, Caroline, whether my uncle Melmoth made any provision for you by will?"

" I believe not! I have been informed he left me wholly to the care of Mrs. Grafton. You know his death, (ever to be lamented) was sudden. I remember the verbal recommendation he gave with me to his sister. Great as my loss was in the death of the best of men, I have never yet had cause to regret my change; as surely, my present patroness has abundantly made up to me that loss."

" I cannot help thinking," said Miss Grafton, " those people very culpable, who take children, and breed them up to the expectation of large fortunes, and dying, think not of making a proper provision for them. Is it not the greatest of all cruelties, to implant notions in their young minds, which they deprive them of the means of gratifying?"

" Had my ever-honoured patron left me to the wide world, or consigned me to the hands of strangers, I question not, he would have secured something to his darling, as he fondly used to style me. But the case is widely different. Mrs.

Grafton ever expressed the highest affection for me, had Mr Melmoth then made me independent, would it not have been tacitly doubting the sincerity of his sister's professional regard for me? In the strongest terms, he recommended to her care his little charge. She promised to act by me as if I stood in the nearest tie of blood to her——She has nobly performed her promise——I can never repay her the moiety of what I am indebted to her, for her hitherto unmerited bounty."

"I wish, Miss Melmoth, with all my heart, you may find that bounty so very extraordinary——What fortune do you reasonably expect my aunt to leave you?"

'Upon my honor, I never once thought of what Mrs Grafton might or would do for me. My affection for her is void of the least mercenary wish. I should despise myself were my heart capable of forming one.'

"Well, but you would not like to be left destitute, after the expectations you have been brought up with."

"I have been left destitute, Miss Grafton. Heaven raised me up a friend—a true one, in Mr Melmoth; he was succeeded by the no less worthy Mrs Grafton. Heaven will never suffer the innocent to languish in misery."

"Very true: but a trifling sum would not suffice to maintain you in the manner you have been brought up. And I must say, unless my aunt meant to leave you an adequate fortune, she has done very wrong."

"It becomes neither Miss Grafton, or myself, to arraign the conduct of the best of women. If she leaves me not a farthing, my obligations to her will be the same——Whatever she leaves me, will be infinitely more than I ought to expect, or can

can merit. But if you please, we will change the subject, as it is one we neither of us know any thing about. May Heaven prolong her much valued life, and whatever becomes of me, I am very indifferent to!"

"Nay, I will change the topic with all my heart, it was for your sake I entered upon it at all. 'Tho' perhaps you will blame my curiosity, but I could not resist the opportunity which offered itself of gratifying it. Mr Shirley, my aunt's lawyer, stay'd dinner, I hinted, I should be glad to know what alterations she had made in her will, he answered, she had made some additions, and reversed some things. You know, I have no more right by law to the fortune of Mrs Grafton, than you have. I was therefore much surprised to hear him say,—he was mighty loquacious—that I was left sole executrix." "Sir, said I, you mistake sure, joint-executrix you mean." "No, no, Madam," answered he, "I know my profession better than to make such palpable mistakes. You are, I repeat, sole executrix and residuary legatee." "May I then ask, Sir, what provision has my aunt made for Miss Melmoth?" "Melmoth, Melmoth," repeated he, "let me see——I remember that name——There are several legacies, Madam." "No doubt, Sir, but to that young lady there must be a very considerable one." "The largest sum mentioned, Madam, is two thousand pounds. And now I recollect, is not the christian name of the lady, Caroline?" "Yes, Sir"—"Well then, she is intitled to two thousand pounds." "Two thousand pounds, Sir!" "Why, Madam, to be sure, two thousand is a large legacy, and yet, it is nothing for Mrs Grafton to leave. She is worth in the funds upwards of fourscore thousand pounds, exclusive of her real estates." "Good God!" exclaimed

exclaimed I, " I thought at least Miss Melmoth would have been left equal to me"

" Which I never did," said I " Blessed, as Mr Pope says, are those who never expected, for they shall not be disappointed"

" Nor shall you, Caroline in me you shall ever find a friend In consequence of my sincere professions, suffer me to apprize you of one thing, but you must first promise me upon your honor, never to let my aunt know, either by word or deed, you are acquainted with what I am going to communicate"

I made no difficulty in assuring Miss Grafton, whatever she pleased to say, should remain a secret with me

" Then," said she, " notwithstanding what my aunt might say to the contrary, your rejection of Mr Davenport gave her great uneasiness"

" I am sure" said I, " I have now under her own hand, a letter, wherein she commends my procedure"

" I know it, my dear, for I persuaded her to write that letter, instead of one she had penned, which, I am certain, would have made you very unhappy She told me, she would not appear to lay any restraint upon you, but that if you had known your own interest, you would gladly have embraced an opportunity of marrying so much to your advantage. and added, I know not when such another will offer he would have taken her without a fortune Mr Blagrave said, he would rather marry you with ten thousand pounds, than any other woman with thirty This I know he said to Mrs Grafton, the last time he made application to her,—to which my aunt answered, the man who takes Caroline Melmoth, must not lay his account to receive much with her At my

death

death perhaps—but I shall make no conditions—
Mr Blagrave then declared, he could not afford
to marry with less."

I answered Miss Grafton, 'Her aunt had an
undoubted right to act as she thought proper in
the disposition of her fortune, the acquisition of
which could not heighten my regard for her, or
the privation of what I had no right to expect
give me any uneasiness."— We then parted

I went into Mrs Grafton's room, where I spent
the night

The only pain I experienced was, that my dear
patroness should treat me with disingenuity Why
would she not frankly write me her sentiments
—Yet could I have complied with her will?—I
ought—I should— nd been miserable!

I am obliged to Miss Grafton for her professions
of friendship, but, I hope I shall never be a dependant upon her bounty She has not those
qualities necessary to render such a state agreeable
With Mrs Grafton, I feel not the weight of dependance My gratitude is infinite, but accompanied with painful restraint

It is true, were my dear patroness to die, the
sum of two thousand pounds is rather a limited
income for one to live wholly upon, who is at present by her bounty surrounded with affluence My
annual stipend, you know, is a hundred and fifty
pounds —But wherever I leave this family, I shall
not have so many wants to supply—and consequently not the need of money as now —My
pensioners will indeed be sufferers, yet, I hope,
as they are good and worthy people, they will
meet other friends with the same will as myself,
and larger power

I yesterday dispatched one of the servants express to Darnley-Crove, as they requested Thank
God!

God! he carries better news than we had reason to expect in so short a time. I wrote to Lady Darnley in a general way. I believe Sir George will sustain a little disappointment, that I did not contrive to send him a note, but I could not think of it. I hope they will shortly come to town. Darnley told me, he should soon have some business which would require his presence. "Of what nature?" I asked. "I know not at present," he answered, smiling, " but if I have not, I shall make some."

It is a strange piece-meal letter I have written, but hope soon they will be more collected. Let me have the pleasure of hearing from you soon. You have not mentioned Miss Arnold lately——My compliments to her. Adieu, my ever dear Sidney.

CAROLINE MELMOTH.

August 5.

Good God of Heaven, my dearest Sidney! Miss Grafton is a vile creature. I know not how even to tell you. I never was in such a tremor in my life. I was going into her dressing-room just now, to speak to her, I opened the door, and, would you believe it? saw her and the infamous Lord L. in the most scandalous familiarity. They started, like guilty creatures.—Well they might.—My God! is it possible, a woman so well descended and educated, can thus degenerate? My confusion, I am sure, was greater than theirs. The wretch, L. I mean, has been here every day since I have been at home, and, I thought, behaved in a particular way to me. I was even afraid he meant to remind me of our childish attachment but that was, I suppose, to cover his shameful intrigue with Letitia.

I declare, I do not know how to see her. How hateful is a vicious character! She too must be conscious I saw her. What must she imagine I think of her?

LETTER XLV.

To Miss VERE.

Grosvenor-Square, August 8.

I Wish I had concealed Miss Grafton's lapse even from you, not that I fear its ever transpiring, but yet, I am sorry I did not bury my knowledge of her indiscretion in oblivion. I believe it was her fault,——at least I hope so. She has discovered to me her long attachment to Lord L. Poor creature! she seems very penitent, and is terribly apprehensive I would acquaint her aunt ——But no more. Do you, my love, endeavour to forget that part of her character, and I will never remind her of it by the least look or intimation.

The impudence of some men is surprising. Lord L. behaves with the utmost freedom imaginable still with the same particularity to me. What does he think I am made of?——But to quit this subject for ever, and advert to a more agreeable one. Mrs Grafton is so much recovered as to ride in the coach, from which she receives great benefit.

She is exceedingly attached to Lord L. and never sees the libertine shine out in his character, as I think

think lately any one may easily. But she has been accustomed to love him from early infancy, and therefore is blind to his faults. I am just going an airing with Mrs. Grafton, excuse this little letter.

I am ever your's

CAROLINE MELMOTH

LETTER XLVI.

To Miss VERE.

Grosvenor-Square, August 14.

THE insolence of Lord L— is insufferable. You cannot imagine how grosly he has affronted me. But, I believe, the repulse I gave his lordship, will free me for the future from his impertinent gallantry: tho' that is too civil a term for the treatment he dared to offer to me.

I suppose these libertines of quality think they have an undoubted privilege to behave in the most insolent manner to those women they imagine beneath them in birth and fortune. I am very ready to allow Lord L— as much superiority as his proud heart can assume, but I should blush to be his equal in one sentiment. Licentious man!

I was sitting this afternoon alone, being prevented accompanying Mrs. and Miss Grafton in their accustomed airing, by an intolerable pain in my head. After reposing myself some time, I found the pain abated, and as I could not go to church in the afternoon, I was very seriously reading some chapters in the bible. Without the previous notice of a loud rap, which generally announces

nounces company, Lord L— entered the dressing-room. I was surprised, not expecting any one.

"Miss Melmoth alone! how fortunate I am! How are you employing yourself?"

"Not in a manner suitable to your lordship's taste, I dare say. I was edifying myself by perusing the best of books extant."

"Then you suppose I never read the bible, but,"——taking my hand, "you are mistaken. There are some very entertaining passages—some droll stories too."

"Are they of no further use, my Lord," withdrawing my hand, "than to excite mirth?" for he smiled at the latter part of his speech. "O yes, very edifying and natural. What think you of the story of Joseph?"

"If you only read it, as an historical passage, it is certainly one of the finest ever penned; but to take it in its true, its religious sense"——

"——It is the arranteft stuff in the world."

"How, my lord!"

"Even so, my lovely Miss Melmoth. Do you now really suppose, there ever was such a man existing, as this same Joseph?"

"I am equally surprised and ashamed to hear such a question from a man, who would be much affronted were his sense to be doubted."

"I do not mean to question the identity of the patriarch, but so far as his story relates to the wife of Potiphar, I think in justice to my sex, I may suppose—or at least—wish it to be apocryphal. A man to act in such a manner, and upon such an occasion, must either be more or less than man."

"I never wish to argue with any one, my Lord, whom reason cannot convince——We will therefore, if you please, drop the subject."

"No,

"No, faith. You seem very capable of supporting the argument——and convincing me too."

"I must despair of it, my lord."

"Cannot you now suppose us in the same situation.—I the virtuous Joseph, and you the lovely Mrs Potiphar.—I think she has no name.—What say you, my Caroline?" attempting to take both my hands. I drew back, and with a smile, said, "I hope I may entertain a better opinion of myself, than the Egyptian lady merited, and I am apprehensive, your lordship would but ill assume the character of Joseph."

"I could not retain it long, I am certain." Gazing on me with ardor in his eyes, I thought he looked odiously.—"Ah! Caroline, you are infinitely too lovely, not to excite inclinations difficult to be suppressed, at least," sighing, "I find them so."

"Then the best method, my Lord, is to withdraw from your presence, since mine involves you in difficulty." I arose. He did so likewise, and stepping before me, said, "Whatever pain you give, you can administer a remedy, but it must not not be by leaving me. No, your charms have kindled a flame in my soul, which the possession of your charms alone can extinguish." During this speech, he snatched my hand, and alternately pressed it to his lips and bosom.

"What mean you, my Lord?"—said I, retreating from him, with a look of surprise and anger. "I hope, I do not understand you."

"I will endeavour to explain myself then," said he. "Know, my lovely girl, I adore you, and unless you will give me hopes, my despair may prompt me to behave unbecoming the respect I wish to pay you."——

"You

" You have forgot that already, my lord: but I will leave you to recollect yourself. I know what is due to me, and for the future shall avail myself of the liberty I have of withdrawing to my own apartment, whenever I meet with disagreeable company. What mean you, my lord, to detain me?—suffer me to pass."

" My sweet girl, even in anger lovely, reject not my suit. By heavens I will be generous to you.—You shall have whatever you please—Half my fortune."

" Insolent wretch! quit the room this moment, or I will acquaint Mrs Grafton with your audacity. I insist, my lord—What right have you to controul my free actions?—I will go."

" By the great God of Heaven," exclaimed the violent wretch, " I will not part with you yet ;" and he absolutely clasped me in his arms, and forcibly kissed my face and neck. Provoked at his horrid insolence, and only sensible to the affront offered me, I struck him a violent blow on the face, somewhere about the mouth, for the blood issued from thence. He retreated back instantly, exclaiming," Damnation seize me, if I forget this! Nothing but the death of a man, can wipe off the disgrace of a blow,—but for a woman—" He stopped, but revengeful ire flamed in his countenance. I trembled, and I am sure was as pale as death. He hastily retired, applying his handkerchief to his mouth, as well to conceal the damage he had sustained, as to stop the bleeding.

I was terrified lest he should take some sudden revenge.

But what can he do? If ever he dares to repeat his insolent offers, I will not fail to acquaint Mrs. Grafton with them. Yet most likely he never

never will, as at least he may know from experience, he has a girl of some spirit to deal with

I remained discomposed a great while. I sometimes condemn myself, as acting very inconsiderately in striking him. Upon my word, it was very fortunate I had no missile weapon in my hand. His attack deprived me of all reflection, and had I had knife or scissars, I might have done him an irreparable injury.

I am tired of writing.—It is late.—Yet I cannot help thinking of this vile lord. He is convinced I think him a bad man, and he seeks to make me a participater in his guilt. What creatures are most of these men! They boast of being lords of the creation——yet glory in being abject slaves to their passions.—As you say, I despise two-thirds of hem.

Your's for ever,

CAROLINE MELMOTH

LETTER XLVII

To Miss GRAFTON

Park-Place, August 14.

HELL confound the little vixen! but I must have her.—I feel I cannot live without her—Yet, what way to gain her?—force nor stratagem I fear will avail;—at least, no stratagem can I think of——Curse on my stupid brain, it us'd to be more fertile, and I am not of an age to have my genius blunted, tho' it has been pretty well employed,——But such rigid virtue!—No catch-

ing at any probability of fuccefs----Devil!----
fhe cannot always be thus cold! Surely, furely, I
have not a rival!--I will have revenge; I have fworn
it Your fex, Letty, never injured me that I
had not ample revenge O, how fweet will it be
to triumph over the haughty virtue of the lovely
Caroline! By Heaven, could I diveft myfelf of my
horrid repugnance to the fetters of matrimony, fhe
is the woman I would prefer to all others But
why do I talk of repugnance? That curfed engagement would deter any woman in her fenfes, from
accepting my hand Do you think Caroline knows
of that damned affair? I hope fhe does not. What
a fool was I, to fuffer myfelf to be drawn into fuch
a fnare!—I thought I could have prevailed on the
fond girl to refign her pretenfions, but fhe had
given my bond to her brother· had I been certain
he carried it about him, his death fhould have put
me in poffeffion of the fatal paper Injured as I
have been, I think I ought to revenge myfelf on
the whole fex

If the dear, bewitching Caroline----fhe is ever
uppermoft in my thoughts---had been a girl of fortune, I fhould not have had half this trouble with
her, but when a woman has nothing to depend on
but her character, fhe is as obftinate as the devil
Nav, I believe had you been poor, you would
have made refiftance

Curfe the blow fhe gave me!---You never
faw a devil look as I did---I was half diftracted I
had a great mind to cut my own throat, rather
than bear the reflection of having received a blow,
tho' from a woman Who can bear the indignity
of tamely putting up a blow? But hold---I do not
put it up fo tamely, no, no, my beloved, vou
fhall dearly repeat that blow

I hurried

I hurried home,---looked in the glafs,---chagrined at the reflection of my difaftrous figure in the mirror, and the ftill worfe in her eyes, I dafhed it in a thoufand pieces---Threw every thing about the room---Curfed my fervants, myfelf, and all the world

My lip is almoft cut thro' I am obliged to wear a patch on it It is violently fwelled I cannot go out, my appearance is fo woeful Heavens! with what force the little virago ftruck! O God! to oppofe ftrength to ftrength, till the exhaufted fair one yields the long contefted prize to my encircling arms!---What rapture does the bare idea raife in my breaft!---But I dare not attempt force, unlefs I had her in a fafe place I will therefore endeavour to fap the foundation of her feemingly impregnable virtue I muft ftrive to conciliate her favor if poffible ---But how?---Aye there's the rub---Let me confider---fuppofe---No It wo'nt do She has too much penetration not to difcover the fallacy, were I to fwear to all eternity I meant but to try her virtue. But if---Faith, I can fix on nothing

I muft fee you if poffible Contrive fome method to come to me I can't ftir from hence--I do not know when I fhall be able to face the fair Broughtonian. Adieu, my deareft Letty believe me ever

Your friend

L

LETTER

LETTER XLVIII.

To the Right Honourable the Earl of L.

Grosvenor-Square, August 15.

WAS I not your lordship's most devoted ally, I should be horrid *chagrin* You have no opinion of your own scheming faculty, and seem likewise to have no reliance on mine But, unsolicited, I will yet assist you

I cannot come to you it would render me suspected; and after the discovery which Caroline has made, it behoves me to be extremely cautious of appearances.

Had I not gathered a few hints from the little vixen, as your lordship styles Miss Melmoth, I should have been puzzled to guess at all your meaning I can make, however, great allowances for your unconnected letter; but very few for your want of spirit, in not humbling the inflexible pride—virtue I will not call it——of Caroline Had you been determined to have taken instant satisfaction for the blow, she,————or I am much mistaken, would rather have given or yielded it, than to have made herself the heroine of such an adventure, and the conversation of the polite circle

I have not time to tell you my plan Think you had better, as you say, endeavour to regain her favor, by appearing a convert to her virtuous sentiments We women love converts of our own making It gratifies our vanity, to be able by our charms to work miracles

The old and not-yet-exploded maxim of reformed rakes, has a wonderful advocate in the breast of most females,---Reform therefore, my
dear

dear Lord, speedily ---but do not over-act your assumed character. Be cautious and happy.

I can no more. I am interrupted. Adieu.

L. GRAFTON.

LETTER XLIX.

To Miss VERE.

Grosvenor-Square, August 18.

I Have no reason to complain of Lord L---'s present behaviour, tho' apprehensive of his vindictive disposition I avoided him as much as possible. He did not pay a visit to Mrs. Grafton for some days, and when he came, he appeared quite another man: a melancholy air, betraying a consciousness of having acted wrong.

I took the opportunity of quitting the room, as his lordship entered. When obliged to return, other company coming in, the chagrin on his countenance shewed he was sensible of my displeasure.

This day he has been here. Mrs Grafton was in her dressing-room, settling some accounts with her steward. Miss Grafton left the parlour to write a letter. As I was determined never to be alone with Lord L. I immediately arose, and was going to quit the room. Lord L. likewise arose, saying, "You need be under no apprehensions, from any future impropriety in my behaviour towards you. I intreat you, madam, to stay, and listen to my sincere repentance, for a fault which a too great sensibility of your charms occasioned. Dare I, Miss Melmoth," putting one knee to the ground, "dare I hope for pardon?

Can that angel-form cover an inexorable heart? Can you, my charming Miss Melmoth, afford pardon and pity to a wretch, so miserable as to offend you, and labouring under the curse of being unable to call you unjust in your anger? Surely, I merit the most rigorous treatment for actions and words---which, rather heated with wine, and my hitherto natural disposition, I was tempted to use to you. Believe me, madam, you cannot condemn me more, than I have done myself, and shall ever continue to do."

"Rise, my Lord, I beg you to rise."

"With transport I would, madam, could I rise with the hope of being forgiven."

"Your future conduct, my lord, will determine mine. I am willing, for my own sake, to give you credit, when you say you were heated by wine. I would not pay myself so ill a compliment to suppose I am capable of inspiring such sentiments as your lordship dared to avow."

"Ah, madam! no one is capable of inspiring purer sentiments than yourself, in a heart under the guidance of virtue and reason. Mine, I fear, has not such monitors to boast. But had I such a conductress as you, I might hope, by adopting your virtuous sentiments, and endeavouring to emulate them, I might not be so very vile a wretch, as, I am certain, I now appear. O, most amiable of women!" respectfully taking my hand, and bowing upon it---"take the heart filled with your idea, under your direction---Turn---dispose it as you see fit, while myself, and whole fortune, I lay at your feet; too happy, if you honor them with the acceptance."

"The repulse, Miss Melmoth, I received for my audacity, gave birth to sentiments, which I never knew before, or never attended to. How amiable

amiable, how truly estimable, did you on reflection appear! New transports filled my soul, at the same time that anguish rent my heart, on the recollection of that mad moment. A new chain of ideas suggested themselves. I arraigned my conduct with the utmost severity. Every part of my life seemed pregnant with some incident, for which I now heartily despise myself. I hope I am not so very bad a man, since my heart is open to self-conviction. Ah! may I indulge the fond hope?———speak, my ever-adorable Miss Melmoth.—Ah! you pause."

" I am never at a loss, my lord, in speaking the genuine sentiments of my heart. If you are become so sincere a convert to virtue, I need not congratulate you upon the happiness I am certain you, and every one, must experience in that heart-felt satisfaction. But, my lord, I must intreat you to indulge no hope."

" Ah! then you will not pardon me!"

" To pardon, my Lord, is in my power, and sincerely I grant it you; but the heart is refractory; it will not in the disposal of itself be controlled. If you deserve my esteem, I will not withhold it,—but more is not in my power."

" I know I feel myself unworthy," said he, sighing—" But reflect, my dearest Miss Melmoth, you have it in your power to save a soul, perhaps from everlasting perdition. Born to the possession of fortune and title, my heart never formed a wish that was not followed by gratification. Left to the guidance of my own inexperience, in a world prone to vice, it is not much to be wondered at, I fell into those snares from which I had no defence. The heart is not, I hope, grown too familiar with vicious courses to be reclaimed, which is sensible

of

of the power of virtue. I am now become a lover of it.—Permit me to say, I love it loving you.

"Ah! do not then desert a man to whom you have just given sight. The glorious prospect you have opened to my view.—guide me by your unerring foot-steps to the heavenly temple. My heart is in your hand,—deign but to mould it at your pleasure."

"Believe me, my lord, it gives me the highest satisfaction to hear you avow these virtuous sentiments.—But do not mistake me, my lord,—there is, I feel it, great difference between esteem and love. The first you may by your good conduct intitle yourself to, but the latter—"

"Ah! then there must be some happy man.— Ah! tell me! ease my racking doubts, by still more agonizing certainty."

"You, my lord, have no right to ask me such a question, or have I an obligation to answer it. You ought to be satisfied in my so readily forgiving your late insult. That is, I think, a greater mark of favor than you are at present intitled to."

"Madam, I acquiesce.—But may I then flatter myself, some time hence, when you are sensible of the character I hope to maintain, you will remit the petrifying looks you have lately beheld me with?—Ah! there was once a time, when those lovely eyes beamed tenderness on the happy Edward. Why! why is it past!"

"That was a ridiculous attachment of childhood, my Lord. I have nothing to plead in excuse for my youthful folly, but the innocent simplicity which constituted the character of Lord L."

"Why!" exclaimed he, clasping his hands, "did I ever forfeit that character?—But it is not too late to be regained."

I thought

I thought this conversation sufficiently long, and begged his lordship's permission to retire — he could not well refuse me, so I hastily left the room,---and sat down to acquaint you with this sudden and marvellous change in the principles of Lord L.

It is very true, as he observed, the nobility are too early made sensible of the consequence which riches and titles give a man in the world. They are likewise taught, all mankind who happen to be born below them are slaves to their will. And if the little lord is indulged in every wish of his heart, he will soon be prompted to enlarge those desires, and to seek all means of gratification.

How much are those to blame, to whom the education of youth belongs!

I mean not to exculpate Lord L from any irregularities he has been guilty of.—I shall be very glad if this alteration in him continues. I own, I apprehended great danger, or at least an attempt of danger, from a man of his enterprising genius, from his violent exclamation and inflamed countenance, in consequence of the blow; but the thorough change in his sentiments renders all suspicion void.

The Darnley family are expected in town every day. I begged Sir George not to write, and after much intreaty, he acquiesced. How inconsistent are the desires of mortals! I could almost breathe a wish, he had not so implicitly obeyed me.

His dear resemblance, which now lies by me affords me great comfort. Adieu, my beloved Sidney.—Your letter is this instant brought me.— I will write to that as soon as possible.

     Your's,
    Caroline Melmoth.
     LETTER

LETTER L.

To Miss Melmoth, in answer to Letter 44th.

Vere-Park, August 13

YOU say, my dear Caroline, I have not lately mentioned Miss Arnold.—I can scarce allow my pen to contaminate itself with the hateful creature. I am half mad. O that you were here, that I might vent my spleen. Don't mistake me neither, Caroline: it is not on you I would vent it, but I can talk faster than I can write. I could storm,—do any thing but cry, and that I am too vexed to do. Would to Heaven I could! I think swearing, now, were I a man, would be a most delightful relief.—But enough of the remedy—now for the disease.

O! that a man can so far degenerate!—And after possessing such a woman too—" who was to this, Hyperion to a satyr."

—Well, but I must determine to acquaint you at once. Yet not to be too abrupt.——I was not, you know, very well pleased with the familiarity of Miss Arnold and William. My prejudices were rather strengthened by two or three circumstances, of which my late maid informed me, and I observed, that if I requested her company to visit or walk with me, she oft pleaded something in excuse.

One day I went into my father's library,——and behold, I saw the sweet pair seated upon the sofa [rather more decently than the virtuous Letitia and her companion] my youthful father's arm round her waist, and holding one of her hands in his other, which he was in the very act of raising to his lips ---They both ſtarted, and looked guilty enough. "O pray don't let me diſturb you," ſaid I; "I am very glad to ſee you are ſuch good company——No wonder you and I have been ſuch ſtrangers lately: your friend William too may complain"——She aroſe at my entrance, and ſtood irreſolute——My father looked very glum.

She murmured ſomething, that my father was alone, and deſired her company—ſhe meant to make ſome excuſe, but I cut her ſhort "Well then, Madam, my father is not alone now; ſo you may go to your own apartment" She left us

"I am very much pleaſed, Sir, tho' equally ſurpriſed, to ſee you ſo well reconciled to a perſon, for whom you expreſſed ſo much diſlike, before you could poſſibly be able to judge whether ſhe deſerved the raſh cenſure you paſſed upon her, or not But ſhe has played her part very well Pray, Sir, if it be not too great a preſumption in your daughter, when am I to have the happineſs of craving her bleſſing as a mother?"

"Why, Sidney, ſhould you ſuppoſe I would marry her?"

"O, becauſe it would be infinitely better than to ruin ſo innocent a creature as this ſame Miſs Arnold——But, Sir, we were both equally right and wrong in our conjectures. I thought her virtuous and unfortunate; you thought her a bad perſon, becauſe recommended by your daughter, who had the fault in your eyes of being deſcended from that bleſſed ſaint over the chimney-piece I know her now to be vile, and you think her worthy to become your wife."

"Indeed

"Indeed you are much mistaken, Sidney. Why---What cause have you to think I would give you a mother-in-law?"

[Now, Caroline, I would have laid a wager of six to four, that every thing was agreed on between them, otherwise my father would have uttered words of resentment at my assurance.]

"I hope not, at least, if ever you do marry, I pray Heaven, it may not be to Miss Arnold. But I have some right over her yet, and believe I can influence her to change her intentions, should she point to the port of matrimony." So saying, I went in search of the heroine of this petit-piece.

After some little preparation, "I told her our dispositions did not agree, therefore I hoped she would look out for some habitation soon. You must be sensible you have not returned the obligations you have received, with gratitude, on the contrary, you are now seeking to do me a very great injury. Yet notwithstanding, I will do you some service out of the house, I cannot consent to keep my enemy under the same roof."

She squeezed out a few tears, and owned my father did make her an offer of marriage.

"And pray, why was not I to be consulted?--- I think I have some right --I am unwilling to remind you, Miss Arnold——"

"---Do you upbraid me with my misfortunes, Madam?"

"No, Miss Arnold, when they appeared such to you, I never did, but it is long since you seemed to think them such, if they ever had existence."

"If I seemed to think slightly of them, Madam, it was for no other reason than that they alone introduced me to the acquaintance and protection of Miss Vere ---"

"---Say,

" ---Say, rather of her father, Miſs Arnold ---But there is ſtill one way left, whereby you ſhall be intitled to my further protection, and at once clear thoſe doubts and ſuſpicions, which I own I cannot help entertaining to your prejudice "

" An unhappy dependant never wants accuſers "

" You wrong me, Miſs Arnold, in the ſuppoſition It ſhould have been your care, by your circumſpect behaviour, to have rendered every attempt of that ſort fruitleſs ---But ſay,---are you willing to keep me ſtill your friend ?"

" ---It would be my higheſt felicity. but that I fear is impoſſible "

" Not at all ſo. The terms are theſe, which if you diſpaſſionately reflect on, you muſt allow to be juſt A woman of delicacy and ſentiment in your ſituation, can never, without forfeiture of thoſe feelings, conſent to marry any one; much leſs ſhould ſhe endeavour to unite herſelf to a family, noble by deſcent, to the utter prejudice of one, who was her only friend Is it thus, Miſs Arnold, you repay me ?---am I thus to be requited for the anger I incurred from my father, by ſuccouring and protecting you ?---I mean not to diſtreſs you---only to ſave you the remorſe a heart the leaſt generous muſt feel on ſucceeding in ſuch a ſcheme---a ſcheme ſo repugnant to honor and friendſhip ---Theſe are my terms---theſe are my reaſons You muſt conſent to quit this houſe 'Till I come of age, and the poſſeſſion of my fortune, I will allow you, out of my yearly income, fixty pounds per annum; as ſoon as I have it in my power, I will make you independent, by ſettling that ſum on you for life, and two thouſand pounds at your own diſpoſal Theſe are articles I will bind myſelf to perform ---They ought, every thing conſidered, to ſatisfy you "

She

She wept ---" They did," she said,---They were as much above her expectations, as they surpassed her desert."

" Then you agree to my proposal?"

" Most thankfully, Madam.-- And the sooner they can be put into execution, the better ---And here," kneeling down, " I most faithfully promise you, I never will apprise Sir William of my retreat, and likewise humbly beg your pardon for my presumption. Your goodness cuts me to the heart." Well, to shorten my story, I was fool enough to believe her promises, and to give her a note of hand of the above

In a day or two, she changed her submissive air for one less becoming, but as the day was fixed for her departure, I did not so much regard it ---But yesterday morning, having desired her to do somewhat, she gave me a very pert denial. " Pray, Miss Arnold, said I, did I hear right?"

" If you heard me say, I should not do your dirty work, did you hear right."

" Then you had better not have owned what you had said."

" I am not ashamed of owning any thing to you, I give you my word."

" Insolent creature! Do you know to whom you are thus impertinent?"

" Yes ---And likewise know it is to one, who owes me respect."

" You!---Respect!"---

" Yes, Madam---the respect due to your father's wife, for such am I."

" Heaven grant me patience! His wife!---Impossible!---"

And out I flew to my wife parent---but he was prepared to receive me.---O, 'tis impossible to

tell

tell you what was faid on all fides Each talking together, and too loud to pay much attention to the other ---But this, among the Babel-confufion, I could hear Sir William fay, " I fhould ftill find a father in him, if I would behave properly, and acknowledge my mother "

" O yes! I will acknowledge her as one of the moft artful, vile---"

" ---Hufh! hufh, Sidney.---She is my wife '---therefore behave towards her with duty and affection."

" With duty and affection! Never, never--- fo help me God!"

My father went up to his bride, who wept plentifully; I wifhed, each tear a drop of fcalding lead ---" Come, my dear love," taking her hand. " I hope this perverfe girl will foon be more reconciled to our union, but however, make not yourfelf uneafy, and confider the title of wife gives you greater claim to my affection than a daughter can "

" I do not at all doubt but I fhall find it fo," faid I " If you, Madam, can find joy, I wifh it you " " You, Sir, will perhaps one day repent a union, which has divided a father and his child At prefent I take my leave of ye both, very unwelcome will the time be to me, whenever we meet."

I retired to my own room, and there received a little relief from a violent gufh of tears I had not fhed one while below, but the fight of my ever beloved mother's picture had that immediate effect upon me Dear departed faint! And muft your Sidney be told to transfer the duty and affection, furpaffing common duty and affection, to another!—the wife of my father!—Forbid it Heaven!

When

When dinner was ready, a servant informed me I told him, "I should eat none" My stomach, Caroline, was full enough. William then came up, with my father's request I would go down, I returned for answer, " I desired to be excused, and that he (William) might never come up to me for the future with any message"

Up then comes my father, who said, " He begged I would come down. I love you, Sidney, and it will become you to behave to me with more temper.—a contrary conduct may alienate the affection I have ever borne to you If you mean not to be an outcast from my house and heart, come down with me."

I was then obliged to go down ---But I could not swallow, tho' my pride prevented a tear from flowing—O, how provoked was I, to give place to her at dinner! Her saucy William seemed to take particular pains to stile her " Lady Vere," and " your ladyship."

I never will go down but to my meals ---My chief time I shall devote to my beloved Caroline, to whom may every wish of her gentle heart be accomplished,, prays

Your

SIDNEY VERE!

END OF THE FIRST VOLUME

THE LADIES,

WHO wish to entertain their Friends agreeably and genteelly, unmixed with Extravagance or Profusion, (if they are not already supplied) are recommended to call in to their Aid

THAT VALUABLE WORK,

THE

Experienced English House-keeper,

Where they will find
The most approved Methods of furnishing the Table with every useful as well as ornamental Article.

This Book contains near Eight Hundred Original Recipts, most of which never appeared in Print.

PART I Lemon Pickle, Browning for all Sorts of made Dishes, Soups, Fish, plain Meat, Game, Made Dishes both hot and cold, Pies, Puddings, &c.

PART II All Kinds of Confectionary, particularly the Gold and Silver Web for covering of Sweet-meats, and a Desert of spun Sugar, with Directions to set out a Table in the most elegant Manner, and in the modern Taste; floating Islands, Fish-ponds, transparent Puddings, Trifles, Whips, &c.

PART III Pickling, Potting, and Collaring; Wines, Vinegars, Katchups, Distilling, with two most valuable Receipts, one for refining Malt Liquors, the other for curing acid Wines, and a correct List of every Think in Season in every Month of the Year.

To which is now added,

An APPENDIX containing above One Hundred approved Receipts in Cookery, Confectionary, Pickling, Preserving, &c And a Copper Plate Print of a curious new-invented Fire-stove, in which any common Fuel may be burnt instead of Charcoal without the least Smoke

By ELIZABETH RAFFALD,

Confectioner, at MANCHESTER

DUBLIN.

PRINTED FOR JAMES WILLIAMS, AT No. 5, SKINNER-ROW. Price only 3s. 3d. bound

Lightning Source UK Ltd.
Milton Keynes UK
UKHW022013310719
347174UK00003B/131/P